Inside
New Zealand
Classrooms

by

Alan Trussell-Cullen

Richard C. Owen Publishers, Inc.
Katonah, New York

Library of Congress Cataloging-in-Publication Data

Trussell-Cullen, Alan.
    Inside New Zealand classrooms / by Alan Trussell-Cullen.
       p.   cm.
    Includes bibliographical references (p.) and index.
      ISBN 1-878450-42-5 (pbk.)
      1. Education, Elementary—New Zealand.   2. Elementary schools—New
Zealand—Cross-cultural studies.   3. Elementary schools—United
States—Cross-cultural studies.   I. Title.
LA2124.T78   1996
372.993—dc20   96–14471
                                                     CIP

"Bayview School Needs Questionnaire" on pages 64–65 © 1994 and reprinted by permission of Instructional Leadership Conference, Auckland College of Education.

"You Can Do It" music and lyrics on page 75 © 1996 by Anne Bradstreet. Permission for reproduction for classroom use only is granted by the composer and the publisher.

"Essential Learning Areas" on page 131 and "Essential Skills" and "Attitudes and Values" on page 132 from *The New Zealand Curriculum Framework* © 1993; "Care of the Bones" from *The School Journal* Part II April 1916 on page 142 and *The School Journal* cover Part Two February 1916 on page 144 © 1916; "New Zealand Teachers' Beliefs About Literacy Learning and Teaching" on page 176 from *Dancing with the Pen* © 1992; "Consensus Beliefs About Teaching and Learning Language" on page 177 from *English in the New Zealand Curriculum* © 1994; all reprinted by permission of the Ministry of Education and Learning Media, Wellington, New Zealand.

Photograph of historic classroom on page 143 reproduced by permission of Turnball Library, Wellington, New Zealand.

Page from *Janet and John* on page 149 © 1949 reprinted by permission of James Nisbet & Co. Ltd., London, England.

Photograph of Sylvia Ashton-Warner on page 150 courtesy of the family of Sylvia Ashton-Warner and reproduced by permission of Auckland College of Education, New Zealand.

Photograph on page 152 courtesy of Elwyn Richardson.

Four poems on pages 154–155 from *In the Early World* by Elwyn Richardson © 1964 and reproduced by permission of New Zealand Council for Educational Research and the author.

Photograph on page 159 courtesy of Don Holdaway.

Photograph on page 161 courtesy of Marie Clay.

RICHARD C. OWEN PUBLISHERS, INC.
PO Box 585
Katonah, New York 10536

Printed in the United States of America

9 8 7 6 5 4 3 2 1

Table of Contents

Acknowledgments

There are many people to thank for their help and encouragement with the preparation of this book. First and foremost, I must pay a special tribute to the five wonderful teachers who allowed me to be a "fly on the wall" and observe all the exciting things happening in their rooms – Kay Greaves, Lesley West, Anne Bradstreet, Martin Turner, and Bev McNaughton. Like all New Zealand teachers, they are also part of a wider educational community and they would not be able to do what they did without the support and collaboration of their teaching colleagues and of course their students – so a special thank you to the children and the teachers at Mount Eden Normal Primary School, and the principals, Frank Dodd and Denis Doyle; Papatoetoe North Primary School and the principal, Philip Cortesi; Bayview Primary School and the principals Bev Barnes and Tim Jenkinson; Leigh Primary School and the principal and teacher Martin Turner; and Howick Intermediate School and the principal Brian Pittams. I would also like to thank Ali Goodall for her help, along with Murray's Bay Primary School and principal Ken Penderton.

Over the years, in my role as teacher-educator I have been privileged to visit many New Zealand schools, to observe and participate in many classrooms, and in so doing, to learn from many fine teachers. In one sense, choosing the five classrooms for this study was not very difficult because there were so many to choose from – but at the same time, that only made choosing the particular classrooms all the more difficult.

My teaching colleagues at the Auckland College of Education deserve special thanks for their help and encouragement with this and all the other projects I seem to get myself involved in.

There are many New Zealand educators who have been an inspiration in my own teaching and I've written about some of them in this book. As a high-school student I read Sylvia Ashton-Warner's novels and in class we debated the issues she raised. She lived close by to the town where I lived and was a figure of both pride and controversy in the local community. I taught with Don Holdaway at Auckland College of Education. At that time I was writing rather weird absurdist stage plays and situation comedies for television. Don suggested, seeing I was involved in education and loved working with children, that I might try writing for children, too. (And so I did!) I knew Elwyn Richardson and visited him in his Auckland school. As a young teacher I studied under Marie Clay and followed her career with professional awe, and I am particularly indebted for the help and encouragement she gave me with this book. A heartfelt thank you to all who have helped mold the way I have come to know and think about learning.

I would also like to acknowledge the help, enthusiasm, and encouragement I had from teachers and administrators in the United States. I have been fortunate to visit many American schools and work with and alongside many fine American teachers. They have helped me come to understand some of the professional and cultural dynamics operating in U.S. schools. They have inspired me with their energy and drive, and their students have enthralled and challenged me as students do everywhere. A special thank you to Ted Fuller (age six) who experienced both U.S. and New Zealand educations and shares his unique insights in Chapter 10.

I would also like to say thank you to the publisher, Richard Owen, for his vision and commitment to education in the U.S., to Amy Haggblom for her enthusiasm and careful "nurturing" of the manuscript through all its stages, and to all who advised and assisted along the way.

Finally, I would like to acknowledge the support of my family and my wife Manon. Life is an educative process and the people you share it with are also your co-learners.

Introduction: Kia Ora[1] and Welcome

At the Auckland College of Education, the New Zealand winter months of July and August are jokingly referred to as the "American season." This is because for the last decade now this has been the time when numerous American teachers have taken the arduous twelve-hour flight across the Pacific Ocean to visit New Zealand and observe New Zealand teachers in action in their own schools. They all come to further their own professional knowledge and understanding. For some the journey takes on almost mythical significance – a kind of pilgrimage in pursuit of some instructional holy grail!

But while New Zealand continues to hold this lively attraction for U.S. teachers, not everyone is able to travel there to see for themselves. That's why I've written this book. It offers U.S. educators and administrators an opportunity to study a number of New Zealand classrooms in action – to meet their teachers, to see how they work with the children, to catch some of the ambiance in their rooms, and to understand and appreciate the philosophy that underlies the teaching – all this without having to travel any further than their local professional booksellers!

In the words of Marshal McLuhan, "Fish don't know they live in water." While "swimming" in these South Pacific waters, we hope as visiting teachers you will not only learn about the New Zealand learning environment, but that it will help you reappraise and even discover new aspects of your own North American educational heritage.

But why should this tiny country thousands of miles away in the southern hemisphere hold such an attraction for U.S. teachers?

To find an answer to that question we need to go back to the 1970s. It was in this decade that research studies that compared how well children were learning in different countries began to push New Zealand into the educational limelight. Suddenly New Zealand teachers found, as much to their surprise as to anyone else's, that they were "number one" in teaching children how to read.

At this time the United States was ranked fourteenth and there was growing public concern about how well "Johnny" (and "Janey")

---

[1] *Kia ora* is the greeting used by Maori, the indigenous people of New Zealand.

could read (National Commission on Excellence in Education 1984). It was not surprising that American educators began to cast their eyes across the Pacific. They wanted to know what New Zealand teachers were doing that was different. The more adventurous began to travel there to see for themselves. At the same time, in growing numbers, New Zealand educators began to visit the United States to speak at conferences and to facilitate teacher workshops. Ohio State University began to introduce Marie Clay's Reading Recovery® Program in 1984. U.S. publishers like The Wright Group, Rigby Inc., and Scholastic Inc. began to sell the books produced by commercial publishers for New Zealand children, while Richard C. Owen Publishers, Inc. began to distribute the New Zealand Ministry of Education's Ready to Read series of books and teacher support material. What began out of academic curiosity was beginning to turn into a kind of revolution.

A variety of names were coined to try to describe what the New Zealand teachers were doing. It was described as "literature-based" – because the children read from a variety of "real" books instead of a single textbook. (After decades of teaching reading without textbooks, New Zealand teachers find the term "literature-based" puzzling – how else do you learn to read books except by reading books?)

The term "whole language" came into prominence, too. It was an attempt to describe the way reading and writing were taught in New Zealand schools as part of a holistic philosophy of learning. This, too, was an American coinage. New Zealand teachers don't talk about "whole" language. They'd probably say: "What other kind of language is there? *Part* language?" In fact, at a New Zealand reading conference, a teacher was reputed to have said: "Hey, the Americans are into something called 'whole language.' We'd better find out about that!"

Like any vogue term, "whole language" initially aroused tremendous interest and endorsement in the United States, but along the way it has also suffered from grave misconceptions and even outright abuse. Teachers frequently construed it as merely an "approach," something that the teacher has to "do." To become a genuine whole language teacher, all that was necessary, it seemed, was to master some new tricks or acquire some gimmicky teaching recipes. For example, there were teachers who thought that just by using big books, they would become metamorphosed into this whole language butterfly. Others thought that all they had to do was expose children to a wide range of real books and by some magical osmosis, they would learn to read and even write – no teaching required! (Readers familiar with *Zen and the Art of Archery* (Herrigel 1989) will recognize a pertinent parallel in all this!)

"Whole language" suffered abuse from the other end of the professional spectrum, too. For some teachers, it was treated with near-religious devotion. By way of example, a few years ago I was invited to give a presentation to a very earnest TAWL (Teachers Applying Whole Language) group. The meeting began with some pious hymn-like singing of a few children's songs, followed by some "readings" for the day from children's books, and finally, I was wheeled in as the preacher with the weekly sermon! (I should also hasten to add that I have spoken to many wonderful TAWL groups where the debate has been lively and the interchange of ideas has been open, generous, and thoroughly down-to-earth.)

Publishers were quick to sense a wind change in U.S. education, too. Even basal textbook publishers began to cynically relabel their new editions as "whole language basals." The inherent contradiction in such a label did not seem to worry them or impede sales (!) and probably shows how loosely people have used the term, and worse, how poorly they have understood it.

In view of the multitude of things being done under this label, it is not surprising that in some parts of the country, "whole language" has been met with something of a community and professional backlash. In this book I have chosen to use the term "language" rather than "whole language" and where a more "global" concept is required, to talk about a *child-centered curriculum* and a *child-centered philosophy of learning*. This is because what we are concerned with here are the beliefs and understandings teachers have about the way children learn. Those beliefs and understandings are fundamental because in turn they determine *the way* teachers teach or their pedagogy and they also determine *what* they teach or the curriculum.

Attempts to implement this philosophy and curriculum in the United States have often been accompanied by intense discussion and debate, not only within the profession but also in the wider community. Of course, this is not only necessary but helpful. But because these changes may be in some measure new to the United States, there is also a tendency to regard them as "revolutionary" and "experimental."

The New Zealand experience can be tremendously helpful here. While the New Zealand model is something that has evolved over time and is continuing to develop, nonetheless its key elements have been accepted and applied for a number of decades. In other words, it has passed the test of time and in fact, in New Zealand – far from being considered "revolutionary" and "experimental," it is regarded as the norm or the standard way teachers teach and children learn. As far as the United States is concerned, what better way to "test" a learning model than to have a whole country use it for 30 years!

But although we talk about the "New Zealand model" – and it is a philosophy of learning that is practiced consistently throughout the country – this is not to suggest that all New Zealand teachers are clones. What I hope to show in the chapters that follow is that there is a core of key beliefs that all New Zealand teachers generally share – a philosophical consensus about how children learn and how best teachers can help them make this happen – but at the same time there is scope for teachers to be different, too. Hence in Part I we visit five different schools and eavesdrop on five different classrooms. All share common goals, but there are subtle differences, too. We will find five teachers with different strengths working with different age groups in different sociological and cultural settings.

In order to gain an overview of the New Zealand elementary school system (what New Zealand teachers call the "primary" school system; see Table 1 on page xii), we will be meeting the teachers in order of the chronological age of the children they teach. In Chapter 1, we start where New Zealand children start their formal schooling – in a "new entrant" classroom. Kay Greaves teaches a class of New Entrants to Junior 2 at Mount Eden Normal Primary School.

Straightaway we encounter a major difference between the two countries. New Zealand children usually start school on their fifth birthday – *whenever that falls in the year*. In fact, a fifth birthday is treated as a very special event. A child's birthday presents are likely to include things like a schoolbag, a lunch box, and pencil sets! U.S. teachers are often alarmed by the fact that New Zealand children trickle into school throughout the year but, in fact, it makes the task of socializing each child and getting them settled in so much easier. The teacher only has to deal with one or two newcomers at a time, and anyway, the main "teachers" for each newcomer are the other children themselves! (New Zealand teachers are liable to find the idea of the U.S. model with the kindergarten teacher having to confront a whole class of "new entrants" on the one day far more frightening!)

The first three years of a child's schooling tend to be rather fluid and the organization of the "junior" classes varies from school to school (as we shall see from the classrooms we visit in Chapters 1 to 3). But usually the beginning child is placed in a "New Entrant" class with other children who are relatively new to the school. After a few months they will be moved into a Junior 1 class (what everyone usually calls

Figure 1. Kay Greaves

a "J1"), and eventually to a Junior 2 class (or "J2"), and then to a class that used to be called Standard 1 but nowadays is more likely to be called Junior 3 (or "J3"). All this may take about two and a half to three and a half years, depending on how well the child settles in, to some extent when in the year the child started, and what best suits the child's learning needs.

Children who have reached Junior 3 will have changed classes at any time in the year. In fact, the movement may sometimes be more determined by how many children are in a class. Teachers from the U.S. with strong mindsets based around "grade level" and children being "promoted" from class to class find this fluid organization rather startling. Actually, the classification does not matter very much to the teachers or the students. In fact, often the children don't even

Table 1		
Age	*New Zealand Class Level*	*Equivalent U.S. Grade*
5	New Entrant/Junior 1	K
6	Junior 2	1
7	Junior 3	2
8	Standard 2	3
9	Standard 3	4
10	Standard 4	5
11	Form 1	6
12	Form 2	7

See Chapter 6 for more information on the New Zealand school system.

know whether they are in J1 or J2 – they are just as likely to tell you they are in Miss Wilson's class or in Room 9.

Furthermore, these junior classes may also be, like Kay Greaves' class – a "multi-age" or what New Zealand teachers call a "composite" class. Kay teaches New Entrants, J1s, and J2s all together in the one classroom (an age span of five years old to seven years old). But all kinds of variations occur in New Zealand schools, such as: New Entrant and J1 composites (together in the one room); or J2s and J3 composites; and even New Entrants, J1s, J2s, and J3s all together in the one composite classroom.

But while the movement through the junior classes tends to be very fluid and may take place at any time during the year, it is usual for all children to start their Standard 2 year at the start of the academic year in February. From this point on, children spend a year in each standard and form level and move up a class level each year. New Zealand teachers like children to stay with their peer group, and so children are not held back to repeat a class or accelerated to a higher class because of their academic progress. Instead, the program is adjusted to meet each child's learning needs. "Composite" or "multi-age" classes are common in these upper grades too. (We visit two in Chapters 4 and 5).

With such a fluid organization and with such a range of ages and abilities in each class it is easy to see why New Zealand teachers tend to think "child-centered" rather than "grade level." It also helps explain the strong sense of "community" in each classroom. Children enjoy helping each other and working together in an atmosphere that is collaborative and cooperative rather than competitive.

Open Plan Classes and Vertical Grouping

There are other organizational models, too. It is quite common to find the junior area organized together for "variable space" or "open plan" teaching. In this case a number of teachers and classes share a large teaching space. There will also be smaller withdrawal areas, and during the day the children will do some things as a total group and some things as separate classes in their own withdrawal areas.

Another model that is not so common but does exist is an entire school that is organized into "vertical" or family group classes in which each class teacher has a multi-age class spanning New Entrant/J1 through to Standard 4 and even to Form 2!

New Zealand parents have a considerable degree of choice when it comes to sending their children to school. In fact, they can send their children to any school they wish, provided the school has room for the child. But in practice, most send their children to the nearest school. By American standards, schools tend to be small – an average school

Figure 2. Variable Space Classroom

Figure 3. Lesley West

would have about 300 students, but many would be smaller than that. As a result, schools tend to be neighborhood schools and in the main the children walk to get there.

Schools also enjoy considerable independence – each is managed by its own Board of Trustees. Board members include the principal, staff representatives, and trustees elected by the parents. (High schools also have student representatives on the board). Being neighborhood schools with a high degree of parental and local community involvement means that schools also tend to reflect their neighborhoods' special qualities and culture. In Chapter 2 we meet Lesley West and her class of J1 children. Her school, Papatoetoe North Primary, is a good example of this. Like every other school in New Zealand it meets all the requirements of the national curriculum, but it is also able to draw strength from its multicultural neighborhood and so develop its own unique character and atmosphere.

Another strength of the New Zealand primary school is the emphasis on teachers being generalists. This means that they are expected to teach all subjects of the curriculum, so the children stay with the same teacher all day. In other words, the class teacher is also the reading specialist, the science teacher, the physical education teacher, the art teacher, the music teacher – and since most New Zealand primary schools teach children how to swim over the summer months –

Figure 4. Anne Bradstreet

even the swimming teacher! Apart from teachers trained in Reading Recovery®, "specialist" teachers are rare in New Zealand primary schools. This emphasis on the teacher as a generalist means that they are able to teach in an integrated way and to help children relate learning in one content area with another. In Chapter 3 we see how a creative teacher, Anne Bradstreet, is able to develop a theme and make it flow into and connect with music, art, health education, so-

Figure 5. Martin Turner

cial studies, science, mathematics, and of course, all aspects of the
language program (oral language, reading and writing, visual language, and drama).

The first three schools we visit are in an urban setting. But what
happens in the country? In Chapter 4 we travel to Leigh, an idyllic
beach settlement, to find out how Martin Turner, a country school
principal, teaches his composite Standard 3 and 4 class as well as coping with the responsibilities of managing a three-teacher school.

At the upper end of the New Zealand primary system children
enter Form 1 and then Form 2. The local primary school may be a
"full primary" and thus take children up to Form 2 or the children
may have to go to a nearby "intermediate" school for these two years
of their education. In Chapter 5 we meet Bev McNaughton and her
class of 37 Form 1 and 2 students, aged eleven to thirteen, and we see
how language is woven throughout the whole day and draws on and
grows through all subject areas.

Figure 6. Bev McNaughton

It is also important to see these five classrooms in their wider context, and that is what Part II is all about. In Chapter 6 we examine in more detail how the New Zealand school system is organized; in Chapter 7, what they teach; and in Chapter 8, how the teachers are trained to teach in this way.

The reader may also be wondering how this all came about. When did it start? How long did it take to develop? Who were some of the movers and shakers? Chapter 9 sets out to answer some of these questions.

Finally we need to sum all this up, and so Part III poses the question: What can we learn from each other? Chapter 10 offers some suggestions as to what a stereotypical "traditional" U.S. teacher might notice in a New Zealand classroom, and what a stereotypical New Zealand teacher might say about a "traditional" U.S. classroom.

But a word of warning about these comparisons. Hear ye who dwell in the land of competition: this is not a contest between the U.S. model (if there is such a thing!) and the New Zealand model. Nor are we suggesting that teachers should try to simply replace one with the other. Our countries have different cultures, different histories, and even a different climate. But hopefully this "visit" to Aotearoa[2] will enable U.S. teachers to see their own teaching in a new light and will motivate them to borrow what is borrowable, adapt what is adaptable, and to value and build on what is valuable in their own schools. To assist with this process, in the final chapter we try to sum up some of the cultural and historical forces that helped make this happen in the New Zealand context in the hope that there may be clues as to how to bring about change and development in the United States.

This book can be read several times in different ways: straight through to gain a vivid picture of New Zealand's education system as a whole; just the classroom and supportive descriptions that pertain to a reader's particular interests and grade level experience; just the sidebars with the decorative borders to gain insight into the nuances of the school system's culture; use the index to clarify terms and support reading other books about New Zealand schools; or scan the photographs to enjoy the "print-saturated" atmosphere of each classroom.

In the last century, when the English settlers came to New Zealand, they brought with them many English birds, including the magpie. Today when out in the countryside one will often hear their plaintive "quardle oodle ardle wardle doodle."[3] But magpies are reputed to have one noteworthy characteristic – they are fascinated by shiny objects and will even go into people's houses to steal earrings and small spangly items of jewelry which they carry off with them and work into their nests. So perhaps the best thing one can do after reading this book is to be like the magpie – take what fascinates you and work it into your teaching.

---

[2] Aotearoa is the Maori name for New Zealand. It is traditionally translated as "Land of the Long White Cloud."

[3] This is a recurring line from a famous poem entitled "The Magpie," by a New Zealand poet, Dennis Glover. It is also available as a children's picture book with illustrations by Dick Frizzell (Glover 1987.)

Part I

⌦⌦⌦⌦⌦⌦⌦⌦⌦⌦⌦⌦⌦⌦⌦⌦⌦⌦⌦⌦⌦⌦⌦⌦⌦⌦⌦⌦⌦⌦⌦⌦⌦⌦⌦⌦⌦⌦⌦

Inside New Zealand Classrooms

Chapter 1

Starting School in New Zealand:
Inside a New Entrant to Junior 2 Classroom

Welcome to Mount Eden Normal Primary School

Figure 1-1. Mount Eden Normal Primary School

Mount Eden Normal Primary School is a city school, close to one of Auckland's many extinct volcanic cones, Mount Eden, or Maungawhau. By New Zealand's standards, the school has a long history. It began back in 1877 and classes were first held in a local church hall. In 1879 the school moved to its present site and the 1879 buildings were maintained until the 1950s. In 1955, the whole school was completely rebuilt, but there are some reminders of the school's history in the war memorial gates that greet visitors as they arrive from

3

the Valley Road entrance and the magnificent mature trees that provide welcome shade in the playground.

A more contemporary addition to the school are a number of large colorful murals that the children have designed and painted.

The Children's Murals

Strong features of the New Zealand classroom are regular "shared reading" and "shared writing" sessions, but art, too, can be "shared," and what better place to display it than on a large, bare, exterior school wall? New Zealand schools do tend to look alike – not surprising since in the past they tended to be built from the same or similar architectural plans – so murals are one way in which schools achieve some noteworthy individuality. Such projects are also an opportunity for the children to claim "ownership" of their schools, and the theme or subject for the mural is usually related to or grows out of some area of the curriculum.

The process of creating the mural is a collaborative exercise and usually involves the following stages:

♦ The class begins by preparing a large cartoon plan which may involve measuring and mathematical challenges to make sure scale and dimensions are accurate.

♦ The children set about creating their own images, working independently or in small groups. These are then put together to form a scaled plan or cartoon for the final mural. This compilation usually is accompanied by much discussion and student evaluation and may require sections to be redrawn or modified in the interests of achieving artistic unity and coherence.

♦ The children's separate images are transferred to an overhead transparency, which is then projected onto the display panel, and the children set about recreating their enlarged image on the panel. Creating the mural on panels like this means that all the work can be conducted in the classroom (regardless of the weather!).

♦ When the artwork is finished it is sealed with clear varnish.

♦ As each panel is completed, the mural is assembled and finally the whole creation is attached to the exterior wall. Usually this is accompanied by some kind of unveiling and celebration.

Mount Eden is primarily a residential suburb, although there is a main shopping area and some pockets of commercial and light industrial activity. The school children tend to come from middle to lower socioeconomic family backgrounds. There is a wide range of ethnic diversity, as well.

Suburban housing in New Zealand usually means a family or a unit of people living in a one-story self-contained house sited on a fifth of an acre of land. But in recent years, as the city's commuter traffic has built up and become increasingly congested, there has been a strong trend toward more high-density housing in inner-city suburbs like Mount Eden. This has meant more apartment buildings (still mostly single story) and house conversions into apartment units.

New Zealand parents have the right to enroll their children at any school they choose, provided there is room for them. When schools become crowded an enrollment scheme must be prepared which sets out criteria for the acceptance of new students. Mount Eden Normal Primary is in this position and accepts students in a defined geographical area. As a result, all the children attending the school live close by. Most walk to school, although a significant number are dropped off at the school by parents on their way to work. No children come by bus and no children are permitted to cycle to school.

School 1: Mount Eden Normal Primary School

Location: Inner-city suburb

School type: A "contributing primary," taking students from New Entrant/Junior 1 (five-year-olds) to Standard 4 (ten- to eleven-year-olds). It is also a "normal" school. This means it is used by the nearby College of Education for demonstration purposes for student teachers in training. (See Chapter 8 for more information about teacher training.)

Roll: 620 students

Staff: Principal, deputy principal, assistant principal, twenty-one classroom teachers, and six additional teachers involved in special programs (such as Reading Recovery®)

School Organization: For organization and management purposes, the school is divided into two areas, the junior department (New Entrant/Junior 1 to Junior 3) and the "standards" – Standard 2 to 4. There are also many activities that help build a sense of a single school community, such as regular whole school assemblies and sharing sessions. Throughout the school all classes are mixed-ability "composites," i.e., they include children with a range of abilities and from at least two class levels with each teacher.

Staff Organization: The teachers are organized into teams and their work is directed by a senior teacher. The junior department is led by the assistant principal and the standards department is headed by the deputy principal. The ultimate responsibility for the running of the school rests with the principal. Teachers have team meetings during the week and the entire staff will meet once a week after school for a whole faculty or "staff" meeting.

Welcome to Kay Greaves' Classroom

It isn't even eight o'clock yet but Kay Greaves is already at school. In the sharing space of her classroom she is preparing her easel for the daily routine discussions about the day of the week, the date, the weather, and the events of the day. At present she has a student teacher from Auckland College of Education with her in the classroom. Kay works with her as a mentor teacher, or as she is termed in New Zealand, the "associate teacher." The student observes Kay's teaching, assists where she can, and prepares and teaches lessons and lesson sequences which Kay will critique. (For more information about teacher training see Chapter 8.)

Soon there will be 37 children in this room ranging in age from five to seven years. As New Zealand children may enter school as soon as they have turned five, whenever that falls in the academic year, some of the children in this class are into their second year at school now and others have only just started. With such a range of experience, individualized child-centered learning just has to be the teacher focus. This affects the children, too: there is a strong feeling of "family" concern for each other. The children don't just learn from the teacher — they learn from each other. There may be 37 children in this class, but there are 38 teachers, and for that matter, 38 learners!

The Class

Class Level: New Entrants to Junior 2
Teacher: Kay Greaves
School: Mount Eden Normal Primary School
Equivalent U.S. Grades: Kindergarten to Grade 1
Years Students Have Spent at School: 0 to 2 years
Ages: 5 to 7 years
Number of Children in the Class: 37
Student Composition:

Ethnicity	*First Language*
25 New Zealand European	English
3 part Maori	English
3 part Samoan	Samoan and English
2 part Tongan	Tongan and English
1 from Serbia-Croatia	English
2 from Korea	Korean
1 from Poland	Polish

From about 8:30 A.M. the children begin to arrive. The children refer to the classroom as their room, and their ownership is evident from the happy energetic way they burst into it. That same sense of proud ownership is evident all about – in the magnificent posters and paintings that hang across the room on strings and cover the walls, in the displays where the children have written about their science projects or logged the growth of their plants from seeds, and in the books and stories they have published and which now share pride of place with the commercially produced reading books and "big books" on display in the classroom.

When the children walk to school, their parents frequently come with them. Often they come into the classroom with the children and stop for a brief chat with the teacher. The children put away their lunches and schoolbags, and also their reading folders. These are plastic satchels in which the children slip a book to take home to read to someone in their family. Included in the satchel is a reading log which lists the books read by the child. Parents are encouraged to hear the children read and sign the record card. The books the children take home are usually the ones they have been reading in the classroom that day so they can be expected to be familiar with the story and able to read it with some degree of independence – one of the aims being to make this home book experience a pleasant and successful one and an opportunity for the parents to share in and celebrate the child's learning.

At 9:00 A.M the children gather in the front of the classroom where they sit on the rug – or what New Zealand teachers call "the mat." Kay sits on a low chair facing them with a small easel beside her. She greets the children with a song in Maori, the language of the indigenous people of New Zealand, and the children join in eagerly. The next song is in English and the children enjoy that, too. In fact, throughout the day the teacher will move from English to Maori and back to English again – a sentence or phrase in one language and then in the other. The children whose first language isn't English know that their home or heritage language is welcome here too.

Now the teacher launches into an action song and the children all join in, using their bodies enthusiastically (movement, music, language, community: holistic learning!).

The children relax and make themselves comfortable again and the class moves on to the normal morning sharing session. The children have items of personal news to tell each other. They talk about the things that have happened at home, about their feelings, about news events, about birthdays, or about the weather. Everyone listens

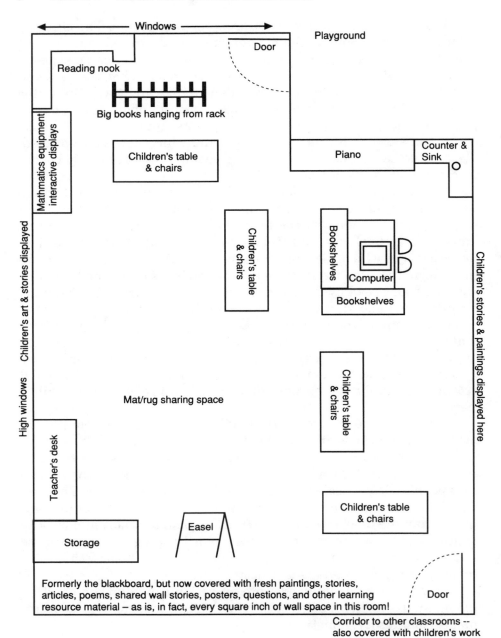

Figure 1-2. Diagram of Kay Greaves' Classroom

intently. Kay is an excellent model, too, listening, asking thoughtful questions, and saying how she feels about what each child has to say. The children follow her example – some even try the same "thoughtful" expression as they listen.

The children are honest and open. Even private experiences are shared.

"Jason was in my dreams last night," volunteers David.

"I hope you had a lovely dream," responds the teacher. Now the

---

The Recognition and Valuing of the Child's First or Heritage Language

A key feature of the New Zealand philosophy of language teaching is the importance of valuing and welcoming the child's first language (or languages). Teachers encourage children whose first language isn't English to use their first language in the classroom – even if the teacher or the other children have no understanding of that language. In fact, when teachers don't know the language, they will then role play the learner and encourage the child to teach them and the other children some key phrases and words in their heritage language. This is partly because language is seen as part of the learner's identity, and valuing what is unique and special about a child builds self-esteem, which is a vital precondition for learning. But it is also a recognition of the important part language plays in the way we think about and come to understand ourselves and the world about us. Many basic concepts will be encoded in that first language, so it is important to keep those active in the child's growing repertoire of concepts and skills.

But what about the child's ability to communicate and use the dominant language – English? As New Zealand teachers shrewdly observe, since English is the language spoken by the child's peers and is the language of power and control in the world they live, of course the children will want to master it, and for the most part, do so very quickly. Instead of trying to replace the first language, teachers work to establish and develop the child's facility in English *alongside and in addition to* the first language.

Figure 1-3. Kay with her class during morning meeting

others talk a little about their dreams. Then one boy talks about going to the hospital to have a checkup for the hole in his heart. The others listen sympathetically. A girl in front of him turns around and stares at his chest for a long time. The discussion moves on but she remains looking at him thoughtfully.

They go on sharing experiences from home and school – there is no distinction. Life is continuous. Sylvia Ashton-Warner would be proud of the heritage to which she contributed (see Chapter 9).

The oral discussion flows naturally into a shared writing experience. The teacher has some sentence beginnings about the day, the weather, and the day's events on a large piece of chart paper clipped to the easel beside her. The children eagerly help the teacher complete the sentences. The teacher tries out her ideas, too, and every now and then she pauses in her writing in order to "think aloud" what she will write next.

Today there is a visitor in the classroom. The children write about him. He is...?

The children volunteer: "big," "smiley," "tall..."

He might be?

The speculations become more imaginative.

"He might be a duty teacher."

"He might be a pilot."

"He might be good at whistling."

What is the New Zealand Teacher's Concept of "Language"?

"Language" for New Zealand teachers is not just about words. In fact, the official English Curriculum refers to three different kinds of language or "language strands" – oral, written, and visual (Ministry of Education 1994a). With these, I like to include a fourth language – that of the body.

In **oral language**, we use a system of culturally significant *sounds* to convey our ideas and we draw on the modes of *talking* and *listening*.

In **written language**, we use a system of significant *symbols* (letters and punctuation conventions) to present our ideas, and we draw on the modes of *reading* and *writing*.

In **visual language**, we use significant *images* and *imagery conventions* (pictures, photographs, video, diagrams, maps, charts, and also typography and layout) to convey our ideas, and the modes we use are termed *presenting* and *viewing*.

With **body language** we use significant *movement* and *gesture* (including facial expression, interactive use of space, dance, drama, and the like), and we convey our ideas by *performing* them and receive them by *watching*.

New Zealand teachers try to explore ideas using a variety of these "languages" or language strands, and frequently one language experience will stimulate and lead into another. For example, the class may read a story, then talk about it, then dramatize it, then draw about it, then write a new story based on the original text, and then illustrate the new story.

♦ Implicit in this is a recognition that children have different learning styles and preferences and a variety of approaches is more likely to touch everyone.

♦ There is also the recognition that when different sense paths are used, an idea is more likely not only to be better understood, but to be more powerfully retained (because it has more experiences to "anchor" it in the memory).

♦ Moving the learning from one language strand to another has a further advantage: it tends to make the children's learning more obvious and to highlight their learning needs. Consequently, teachers can observe and assess and evaluate the learning as they go along in a much more natural and organic way.

"He might be a poet."

"He might be a sailor who goes around the world."

When teacher and children have finished their writing, they read it over together. Now the teacher uses a plastic pointer to make sure the children associate the spoken word with the written form. The teacher then chooses a child helper to point to the words and they read it through again.

The whole first half of the morning in this classroom is a "language block." The children will use language to speak, listen, write, read, think, and share their ideas. They will also draw and use their bodies to express their ideas.

The time scheduling for these activities is very flexible and open-ended. Some mornings the shared writing may take longer and sometimes not. If the morning discussion fires up intense interest in something, the teacher will use that teaching moment to extend the learning. The same may happen in the shared writing – sometimes this may take ten minutes, sometimes twenty, depending on the children's responses and needs as observed by the teacher.

But if the time scheduling is flexible, the structure and sequencing for the morning remains constant: oral discussion flows into shared writing, which then moves naturally into individual writing. After the morning break, this language momentum carries the class into reading and related experiences. Children need flexible "learning time," not the confines of mechanical "clock time," but they also need the security of a predictable pattern.

Typical Daily Schedule

9:00 – 10:15	Oral and Written Experiences
10:15 – 10:35	Class Mathematics Experiences
10:35 – 11:00	Break
11:00 – 12:30	Reading and Related Experiences; Korero Sessions (discussion incorporating Maori language)
12:30 – 1:30	Lunch and Break
1:30 – 3:00	Theme (Language/Art/Social Studies/Science/Health/Music)

Variations to Daily Schedule:

Time for:

♦ Te Reo Maori Enhancement classes (A substitute teacher takes Kay's class while she works with a group of children drawn from the junior classes who have been identified by their parents as of Maori heritage to study and improve their use of the Maori language.)
♦ Library sessions

♦ Junior sports (involving seven classes)
♦ Physical Education
♦ Swimming in the summer months
♦ Team Assembly (Thursdays 1:20 to 2:15)
♦ School Assembly (Fridays 10:00 to 10:40)

Reading and Writing: Approaches to Instruction

With reading and writing so intertwined and interrelated in the New Zealand classroom, it is not surprising to find teachers using similar terminology to describe the main approaches used in reading and writing instruction. Just as reading will involve read-tos, shared reading, guided reading, and independent reading, so in writing instruction the children will be written to, experience shared writing, and participate in guided writing and independent writing.

Reading	Writing
Read-to Experiences The teacher reads to the children to model the process and to help develop a love of books and an appreciation of the usefulness and the pleasures of being able to read. Unlike shared reading, in a read-to experience, the teacher takes the full responsibility for the text; the children do not have to see it. Reading to students of all ages exposes them to new genre and language and creates a feeling of being part of a reading community.	*Write-to Experiences* The teacher writes in front of the children to model what life-long writers do. The teacher's demonstrations, while originating from a personal list of topics, are selected on the basis of the identified needs of the learners. For example, while looking at the children's draft writing books, a teacher may have identified that a number of them seem not to be using their plan for writing. In a write-to experience, the teacher demonstrates such a list and then talks aloud during the draft process to show how to attend to the list while writing. The teacher models the writing process, and through engagement and a carefully identified objective, assures that learning is occurring.

(Continued)

Reading	Writing
Shared Reading	*Shared Writing*
The children follow text with their eyes while they receive voice support. The support most often comes from the teacher, but can also come from a taped reading. An enlarged text, a big book, or individual copies of books are tools that can be used. While the teacher still takes the primary responsibility for the reading, the children are encouraged to join in when they feel comfortable. This approach allows students to participate in the reading process with text that may be too complex for them to read independently.	This approach, also known as *language experience,* involves a shared experience which provides the basis for thinking, talking, writing, and reading. The goal is to help learners understand that "what has been experienced can be talked through, that the talk can be written down, that the writing can be refined, and finally read by others" (Ministry of Education 1992, 109). The class may share an event. The teacher acts as scribe while the students talk about what they have shared. The writing is published in some format so it may be read and re-read by the students and others.
Guided Reading	*Guided Writing*
The teacher works with a group of children to help them "talk, read, and think their way" (Ministry of Education 1985, 69) through a selected text. A small group of children is brought together for a specific need based on a carefully evaluated assessment sample (such as a running record). The texts selected provide sufficient supports to scaffold new learning, but contain too many challenges for these children to read on their own. With individual copies of the text, the children read silently with guidance from the teacher. The purpose of this approach is to develop the children's skills for strategies they can use to create meaning when reading independently and as life-long readers.	The teacher monitors children's writing closely (one-on-one or in a small group) to ensure that learning continues. These sessions can occur at all stages of the writing process, based on the needs of the learners. One form is the editing conference, in which a student who has revised and proofread a piece places it in a box labeled "I am ready for an editing conference." The teacher first reads the piece, noting the strengths, what the writer can do, and what the next learning step is. Then the teacher and student meet one-on-one for direct teaching of the next step. Another form is the small group conference, in which students can conference at any stage of the writing process, from topic selection to planning to revision.

(Continued)

Reading	Writing
Independent Reading Daily, children should read texts that contain no challenges they cannot overcome by themselves. With younger children, the teacher may identify through running records about 30 texts they can manage, which are placed in a book box to be shared with four or five other children at the same level. Older children self-select texts for their own purposes. The teacher may provide roving conferences and may observe and record reading choices, attitudes, and significant reading behavior.	*Independent Writing* A time is set aside daily for writing. The children work independently. Most often, topics are self-selected, but occasionally a teacher may assign a particular genre to older learners. With the goal of publishing, the teacher will provide roving conferences, assist the writers when necessary or when it will be productive, and observe and record significant writing behavior and learning needs.

So as the shared story writing comes to a close, the children are already anticipating the next stage of the morning's language journey: writing their own individual stories.

The children have draft books, or what New Zealand children call "exercise books," in which they now begin to write on their own. While the children write, the teacher and the student teacher conduct roving conferences. They move around the class, conferring with individual children and giving help and support. There is a workshop atmosphere in the classroom with everyone "on task," as New Zealand teachers are fond of saying.

The five-year-olds who have only just started school may draw their ideas, and then with a mixture of recognizable letters and letter approximations, try to convey their meaning. Their writing may contain approximations but it is also real writing, and the teacher receives it with the respect good readers show real writers. As she reads it with them, she constantly praises and endorses the child's achievements: "A party! That's lovely! And you've got the *p* and the *t*! I'm really impressed!" The teacher puts a big check over each correct letter to reinforce this. (In New Zealand it would be called a "tick.") At this

Figure 1-4. Child writing in draft book

stage the teacher may also scribe the correct spelling of some of the key words for the child.

As Kay reads and observes and works with the children, she notes clues as to where children are in their own development and where she can best help their emerging writing expertise. She also keeps samples of their writing to document their progress and stores them

---

Making Assessment and Evaluation "Authentic" and Relevant to the Learner

Our best policy is to monitor actual behavior as the child carries out the task in a meaningful situation – such as normal reading and writing within the program – and to compare such observations with those taken for the same child at some previous time (Holdaway 1979, 168).

Stages of Spelling Development

New Zealand teachers have found Richard Gentry's five stages of spelling development very useful in assessing and evaluating children's progress. The following examples from Kay's class help illustrate these stages:

Precommunicative

This is Julian's first day at school and like everyone else, he writes a story. He expresses his ideas using visual language – he draws – and the teacher publishes it for him.

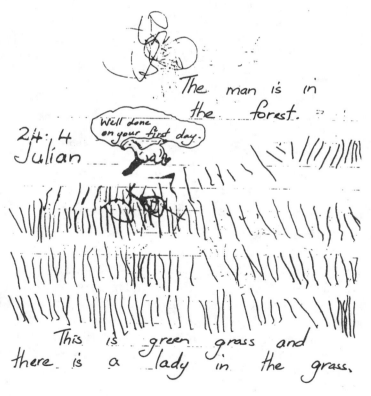

Figure 1-5. Julian's Piece

(Continued)

Figure 1-6. Harry's Piece

Harry is a little further advanced. He shows some knowledge of the alphabet as letter forms but no awareness of letter/sound relationships. He has written his letter forms in lines and shows an understanding of the left-to-right principle of directionality. There is also a mix of upper- and lowercase letters with a clear preference for upper case, which is common at this stage.

(Continued)

Semiphonetic

Adam is beginning to grasp the idea that letters have sounds which represent the sounds in words – and he is very successful when assisted by the teacher with the word *microphone*. Typical of this stage, he also makes use of partial phonetic representation of some words (e.g., *w* for *went*). He has greater control over letter forms, too, as shown by his use of lower-case letters. The teacher has written *Ka pai*, meaning *well done* in Maori.

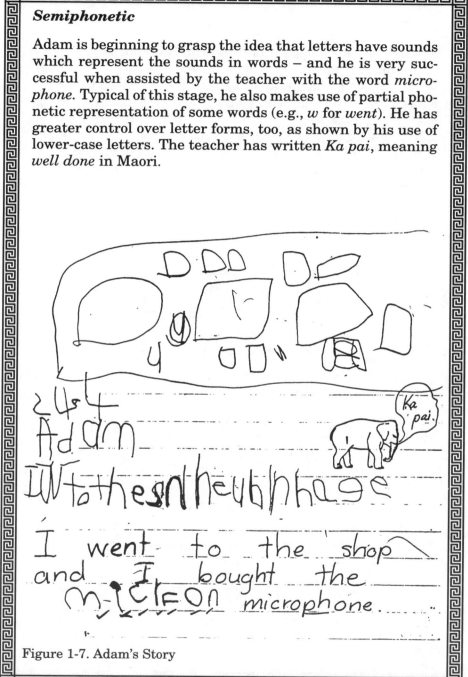

Figure 1-7. Adam's Story

(Continued)

Phonetic

Francis has very carefully and accurately mapped out the letter-sound relationships in the words she has used. She writes letter forms primarily according to the sounds she hears rather than following the conventions of English spelling (e.g., she writes *mi* for *my* and *gtn* for *getting*). But she is clearly aware of word spacing and the left-to-right principle of directionality and she also displays a mix of stages, with some correct spellings (*am* and *for*) besides the semiphonetic and phonetic spellings.

I am going to get a bike for my birthday. I am getting a stand on my bike.

Figure 1-8. Piece by Francis

(Continued)

Transitional

Kate is moving from a heavy reliance on sound to represent words to a greater reliance on analogous spelling patterns. Her syllables all contain vowels now, she uses nasals before consonants (*and*, not *ad* or *adn*, and *went*, not *wet*), and there are many words she obviously knows by sight (*mouse* and *zoo*).

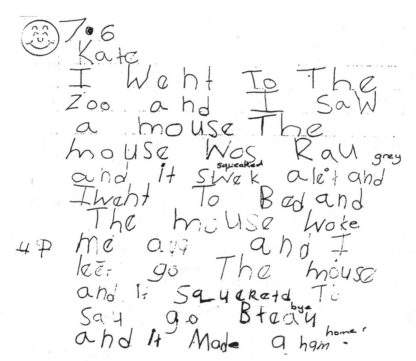

Figure 1-9. Piece by Kate

Correct

At this stage, the writer has a large body of known words, can use prefixes, suffixes, contractions, and compound words, is gaining greater control over irregular English spellings, including silent consonants, is able to suggest alternative spellings when unsure about a word, and can use spelling resources such as a dictionary, thesaurus, or spelling checker.

(Continued)

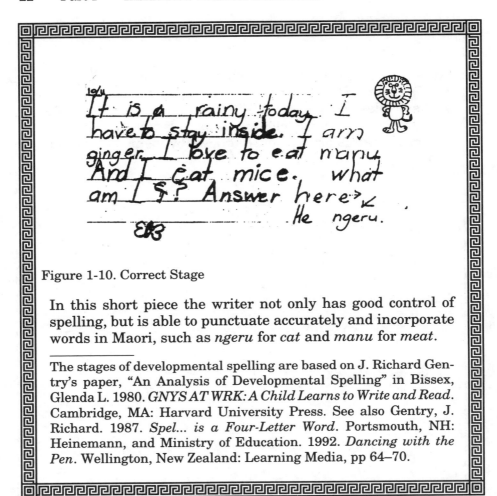

Figure 1-10. Correct Stage

In this short piece the writer not only has good control of spelling, but is able to punctuate accurately and incorporate words in Maori, such as *ngeru* for *cat* and *manu* for *meat*.

The stages of developmental spelling are based on J. Richard Gentry's paper, "An Analysis of Developmental Spelling" in Bissex, Glenda L. 1980. *GNYS AT WRK: A Child Learns to Write and Read.* Cambridge, MA: Harvard University Press. See also Gentry, J. Richard. 1987. *Spel... is a Four-Letter Word.* Portsmouth, NH: Heinemann, and Ministry of Education. 1992. *Dancing with the Pen.* Wellington, New Zealand: Learning Media, pp 64–70.

in a personal portfolio for each child. With each piece she makes anecdotal notes: she records the title of the piece, the date it was completed, and any learning milestone exhibited in the piece or learning need it suggests. She will also classify these milestones or needs, not in terms of a "grade," but as belonging to one of three stages of developmental maturity described as follows:

- ◆ "can do this now" (or "is doing this consistently") or
- ◆ "is starting to do this now" (and may need some help and support) or
- ◆ "is not doing this yet" (and may need some introductory help).

At 10:15 A.M., Kay begins to sing. She uses a tune they all know (this time it is "Skip to My Lou"), only she makes up the words as she goes along because she is really instructing the children to put their writing books away and come to the mat for mathematics.

> *Well now* tamariki (Maori for children) *come to the mat;*
> *Well now tamariki, come to the mat;*
> *Well now tamariki, come to the mat;*
> *Let's all sit together.*

This is a common management technique used by New Zealand teachers. Often it will be in the form of a question and answer:

Teacher: Where are my tamariki?
Children: Sitting on the mat.
Teacher: Where are my tamariki?
Children: Sitting on the mat.
Teacher: Where are my tamariki?
Children: Sitting on the mat.
Teacher: Now we are ready for maths! (In New Zealand the teachers abbreviate mathematics to math*s*.)

Mathematics at this level is taught using a resource called *Beginning School Mathematics* (Ministry of Education 1994b). Teachers generally refer to it as BSM. (It is also used with great enthusiasm in parts of the United States.) The emphasis is on experiencing key mathematical concepts through shared experimentation, practical activities, and real life experiences. BSM is also a rich *language* program. The children are constantly encouraged and challenged to talk about their math ideas and discoveries.

Today Kay begins by asking: "I wonder if we have more boys or more girls in the class. How could we find out for sure?"

"We could count them."

"Yes, we could."

"We could make lines and see which is the biggest."

The teacher is impressed: "We could make lines, couldn't we, Matthew? I think we should try that." Now the teacher organizes the boys in one line and the girls in another. There are really more girls than boys but she arranges the lines so that the boys' line is more spread out. "Well, look at that – there seem to be more boys than girls!"

The children aren't fooled by this: "But they've got bigger gaps!"

"So they have. Well, what are we going to need to do if we're going to compare these two lines?"

"We'll have to match."

"Right! We'll have to *match*, won't we? We'll have to match a girl with a boy to make sure we are being fair..." The teacher helps them match up a boy and a girl. They talk about the number of children left

over. They talk about "greater than" and "less than." There is new vocabulary, new concepts, new ways of using the words they know. She
follows this with other matching and grouping activities.

"How many people have some blue in the clothes they're wearing
today? How many have some red? How many children have one
pocket? How many children have two pockets...?"

This discussion and activity lasts only five minutes. On the task
board the teacher has a range of individual activities for the children
to do and there are optional activities for children who have finished
all their assigned tasks. The teacher now sends the children off to
work on these. She doesn't have to tell them what to do – they can
read it for themselves! In a few seconds they have the equipment they
need and are hard at work. Meanwhile the teacher works intensively
with one group, then moves to another group and so on...

At 10:35 A.M., Kay begins to sing again. The children pack up their
equipment and gather on the mat. The teacher picks up her guitar and

---

The Importance of Empowering Attitudes

The teacher chooses Rebecca's story (see page 27) for two reasons – partly because it is a good story and she knows the children will enjoy it – but also because she has been observing
Rebecca's progress in reading and she wants to help her with
a motivational boost. This is clearly "authentic assessment" at
work. New Zealand teachers prefer to assess and evaluate children's learning while it is happening rather than using tests
(where instead of being "authentic" or "natural," the behavior
being evaluated has to be artificially simulated). In their assessment and evaluation they look at three things:

♦ Knowledge and understandings (What does the child know
  and understand, or need to know and understand now?)
♦ Skills and strategic behaviors (What can the child do or need
  to be able to do now?)
♦ Attitudes and values (What does the child feel about the
  learning and how do the attitudes and values that cause
  these feelings help or hinder the learning?)

The motivational boost for Rebecca is clearly to help in this
last area.

strums some chords. They launch into a favorite song. The bell rings and they are dismissed for what the children call "playtime" and the teachers are more likely to call "morning tea," "break," or "interval."

At 11:00 the bell sounds again, and the children make their way into the classroom. They know what happens next, and without having to be told they gather up a book, take a poetry card, or unhook one of the big books from the stand and start a period of independent reading, what they call "sustained silent reading" or SSR. Some children remain sitting at their tables. Some stretch out on the floor. A small

Independent Reading

This is a daily period of independent reading when the children are able to choose whatever they wish to read. The purpose is to establish reading for pleasure as a normal daily activity and to encourage children to make personal choices about what they would like to read. In order to model and give his or her stamp of approval, the teacher may participate for some of the time, too. After a few minutes of modeling, the teacher may then quietly put her own book away and rove to observe what the children have chosen to read. Teachers may also use this time to complete a running record.

The activity needs to be regular (preferably daily), sustained (i.e., for sufficient time to make it a worthwhile experience for the children), silent (so everyone can concentrate), and involve *reading*. Teachers often find it is a useful "calming" or "mood-setting" activity to do after periods of vigorous excitement, such as after lunch- or playtime breaks. It is also an activity that is valuable with all ages. (Secondary school English classes in New Zealand will often have a regular period of independent reading.)

It is usual for the teacher to conclude the activity with a minute or two of "book talk" – some sharing of responses and reactions to what they have been reading and the chance for children to "sell" something they've really enjoyed.

Teachers sometimes refer to the activity as *sustained silent reading*, or SSR, although children do not always understand acronyms: I recently asked a six-year-old what SSR stood for and he said: "Super Silent Reading!"

group curl up with their books in the classroom library corner. The teacher has her own book, too, and like the children she gets comfortable and settles down to read – the teacher as model.

After a couple of minutes Kay puts down her book and begins to rove quietly around the room, noting what the children have chosen and how they are reading. Now she calls them to the mat.

Browsing Boxes for Independent Reading

These are boxes of books with assorted titles with which the children have already had some experience. The boxes are color-coded and correspond to texts for emergent readers, early readers, and fluent readers. U.S. teachers might call these "book boxes."

- **Emergent readers** are making a start; they are interested in attempting to read the text unaided, are able to talk about what is happening and what is likely to happen in the story, and will create meaning from texts appropriate to their level of reading development.
- **Early readers** are paying closer attention to the meaning in the text. To do this they will draw on background experience; take risks and try approximations; use words and illustrations to sample, predict, and confirm their predictions; use letter-sound associations to check out their predictions; show some knowledge of print conventions; are able to re-read or read ahead when they have lost the meaning; self-correct; and are beginning to integrate different meaning-making strategies in what Marie Clay calls a "self-improving system."
- **The fluent reader** is able to go it alone, has confidence, has integrated cues, can read longer and more complex sentences and different kinds of writing and still maintain the meaning, and rather than mechanically checking out all print detail, selects what is needed to gain meaning and can vary the rate of reading to meet the purpose.

(For a fuller description of these stages, see Ministry of Education 1985, 86–87; and Mooney 1988, 7–11.)

Reading Around the Room

The children really enjoy this activity. Usually they will do this in pairs, not because the teacher has told them to do it that way but because that seems a natural and pleasant way to do it. They move around the room and one child will read some wall text out loud to the other child, and then they will change roles for the next piece of wall text. Sometimes the children take a plastic pointer with them and one child will point to the text while the other reads. (The pointer is made of soft plastic so it is not likely to cause injury if anyone is poked with it! It is also curved rather than straight. This means it does not cover or mask the text being read.) This activity works so well because New Zealand classrooms are rich in displayed text. In fact, one visiting American teacher described New Zealand classrooms as "print-saturated."

"You've all been reading so well, and I saw some of my favorite books being read today. Rebecca had one of my favorite stories, didn't you, Rebecca? If she doesn't mind, I'd like to read her book to the class this afternoon in story time. Is that all right, Rebecca?"

Rebecca is delighted!

The teacher now draws their attention to the reading task board. There the children can see their names on magnets attached to the board, and alongside are the activities the teacher has chosen for them for today. Some are reading books from the browsing boxes. Some students will be working with alphabet activity cards. Some will be reading around the room. A small group will read with the teacher and do some close study of the text and discussion of reading strategies or *guided reading*. One group of children listens to a story on tape and has individual copies so they can follow the text. Another group will be choosing from the big books. Some children have free choice, meaning they can choose any of the normal reading activities. These groups are not fixed. The teacher will organize a group for today because they have common needs or she wants them to do some intensive work with her – but tomorrow or next week the same children may be working with others on quite different tasks.

The children work through to 12:15 P.M. Throughout that time the teacher has managed to do some intense discussion with two groups of children, has circulated round the others and observed what they are doing, and has even found time to sit down with a child to hear and observe him reading a familiar text in order to take a *running record* (an analysis of what the child does when reading). The teacher notes words read correctly in the text and in particular observes what the child does when unsure about a word or gets a word wrong. This is a major source of reading evaluation data. At this stage, in order to keep a close watch on their reading progress, New Zealand teachers generally do a running record on each child about every three weeks.[2]

Lunchtime is at 12:30 P.M., but Kay brings the class onto the mat a few minutes before that and together they share some of their favorite poems. These are on large teacher-made cards. The teacher calls on child helpers to hold them while they all read together.

Figure 1-11. Kay taking a running record

[2] For more information about running records, see Ministry of Education. 1985. *Reading in Junior Classes*. Wellington, New Zealand: Learning Media, pp 121-131 and Clay, Marie M. 1993a. *An Observation Survey of Early Literacy Achievement*. Portsmouth, NH: Heinemann, pp 20-42. The latter title and *Reading Recovery: A Guidebook for Teachers* (Clay 1993b) replace *The Early Detection of Reading Difficulties* by Marie M. Clay.

RUNNING RECORD SHEET

Name: *Andrew*   Date: 27· 3· 91 D. of B.: 3· 12·84 Age: 6 yrs 3 mths
School: *Mt Eden Normal School*   Recorder: *McGreaves*

Text Titles	Running words Error	Error rate	Accuracy	Self-correction rate
1. Easy _____		1: _____	_____ %	1: _____
2 Instructional *Rain Rain (RtoR) (seen)*	58/4	1: 14	93 %	1: 5
3. Hard _____	_____	1: _____	_____ %	1: _____

Directional movement _____ ✓

Analysis of Errors and Self-corrections
Cues used or neglected [Meaning (M) Structure or Syntax (S) Visual (V)]

Easy _____

Instructional *Andrew used meaning structure and visual cues in three*
of his attempts. On page 4 (up to the error) cook could have used
Hard *structure but he then re ran and changed the structure.*
_____

Cross checking on cues (Note that this behaviour changes over time)
He didn't cross check with visual cues
his attempt Puddle / stream

Analysis of Errors and Self-corrections
(see *Early Detection* page 21)

Page	Rain rain (Ready to Read)					E	SC	E MSV	SC MSV
2.	✓R	✓	✓	✓	tracks / track	1		(m)(s)(v)	
	✓	✓	✓	✓	✓				
3	✓	✓	✓	✓	✓				
	✓	✓	✓	✓	✓				
4	✓✓	cook |sc / cooked|	✓	✓		1		(m)(s)(v)	m(s)v
	✓	✓	✓	✓	✓				
5	✓	✓	✓	✓					
	✓	✓	✓	✓					
6	off |A /T	✓	✓	✓		1			
	✓	✓	✓	✓					
	✓	played |A / paddled|T	✓	✓	puddle / stream	2		(m)(s)v / (m)(s)v	

Figure 1-12. A running record

Lunch in New Zealand Schools

Unlike most U.S. schools, New Zealand schools do not have lunch cafeterias. Instead, the children bring a bag lunch from home and usually eat it outdoors if the weather is fine. When the weather is cold or wet, the children eat in their classrooms. As a fund-raising program, in some schools parents run a voluntary lunch-making scheme for children who wish to buy their lunch.

The lunch bell sounds. The children collect their lunches from their bags and gather outside the classroom. Some sit on the outdoor seating and others sit clustered in front of them on the concrete. The children from the other classrooms in this block are doing the same outside their own rooms.

It is a warm, fine spring day. The children munch the sandwiches they have brought from home and chatter happily while the duty teacher moves among them, talking to this group, saying "Hi," to a child here, a child there. Meanwhile, Kay has joined the other teachers in the staffroom. The whole school stops for lunch at the same time so apart from the two teachers on duty, all the staff gather together for lunch.

After fifteen minutes the duty teacher lets the children go and play if they have finished eating. Most rush off to the grass playgrounds. Some collect a large rubber ball from the classroom and begin a game of four square on the concrete. Some are soon hanging upside down on the climbing frame. Lucy and her friends remain on the outdoor seating, gossiping about a television program they watched the night before.

When the teachers have finished eating their lunches, some make their way back to their classrooms to do some preparation for the afternoon session. Others wander out into the playground to talk to the children and maybe join in a game if invited.

At 1:30 P.M. the bell sounds and the children calmly make their way back into the classroom. Game equipment is put away and the children gather on the rug where Kay is sitting waiting. As promised, she has Rebecca's library book to read to the class. (This is a read-to experience – see page 13.) She begins by asking Rebecca why this is her favorite book at the moment.

"Cause I have my own copy at home," she says, visibly growing taller with this special attention.

The children snuggle into a comfortable position and the teacher begins to read. Every now and then she stops and "wonders" out loud about something in the story. The children eagerly respond. Of course, she is questioning and subtly checking on their understanding as she goes along, but it is all very natural and relaxed. There are no "wrong" answers, either. She receives unlikely responses with comments like:

"That's an interesting way of putting it..."

"I've never thought of it like that, Francis..."

"Oh yes, it might be. On the other hand..."

Unexpected responses receive particular praise:

"What a wonderful idea!"

"Oh, that really makes me think!"

If this was a photograph and one was looking for a caption, a good one would be: "We all love this book!" or just "We all love reading!"

The story takes about ten minutes. The book is then returned to Rebecca, who proudly takes it and puts it with her things. If Rebecca loved the story before this, it has even greater significance now!

The rest of the afternoon is devoted to an ongoing theme study that integrates content from two curriculum areas: social studies and health education, but also draws on art, music, drama, poetry, and of course reading and writing and lots of discussion. The social studies theme is titled "appreciating differences," while the health topic is "relating to others."

The teacher begins by drawing the children's attention to the shared story they wrote in the morning. "Today we have a visitor in our classroom, don't we? And this morning we were wondering who our visitor was and what was special about him. You thought he might be a duty teacher or a pilot. Josie thought he might be a sailor who goes around the world! That was a wonderful idea, Josie." Josie smiles and proudly rocks to-and-fro. "But now I want us to think about each other. I think it would be lovely if we really got to know each other. That way we'll be able to help each other and we'll all have friends. What's a good way to get to know someone?"

"Talk to them?"

"Yes. If I wanted to know all about Ryan, that's what I'd do. I'd sit down with him." The teacher puts a chair alongside hers and motions Ryan to come and join her. "Then I would ask him questions like... Mm... What could I ask Ryan?"

A LONG TERM PLANNING FORMAT

CURRICULUM AREA Health from a Social Studies Aspect. PERIOD FROM Wk1 T3 TO Wk2 T3 Tue, Wed, Tue, Wed.	**ORGANISATION/PREPARATION FOR LEARNING** Wk1. Class. Into pairs. Report back to Class. Pairs - illustrate - caption. Wk2. Class. Groups at tables, and Floor Area
GROUPINGS Wk1. Class. Pairs. Wk2 Class Groups at work areas in the classroom.	**RESOURCES** Poem: "People Are Different." Insight Series. Healt unit. Being Friends Children themselves. Paper, pencils, felt pens / sketching pencils. P.11, 12, 13 (Wk1) P14, 15, 16, (Wk2)

	EXPECTED LEARNING OUTCOMES	LEARNING ACTIVITIES
Wk1 Tue + Wed	Children practise getting to know about one another, thru' questioning, answering, reporting, illustrating, and writing.	- Teacher motivates session - Chn respond to instructions. - Chn move to quiet area in pairs. - Tchr interacts, observes as chn tell each other about themselves. - Chn practise introducing each other once they have sufficient information. - Each pair reports back to Class grp. - Class audience listens to report backs + acknowledges efforts. - Captions are written by chn if able to, or by Tchr. to accompany illustration by person doing introduction.
Wk2 Tue + Wed	Children take part in a group activity requiring co-operation and trust and talk about the experience afterwards.	- Tchr sets scene for "Listening + Looking Game". - One child leaves room - Object chosen and hidden. - Class response - loud soft clapping. - Repeat the game to reinforce points that emerge from discussion. Refer (p14) - Tchr sets scene for "Listening Without Looking." - Trust. Blindfolded. - Discussion - Refer (p14 + 15)
	The children practise some of the skills of co-operation such as being considerate, sharing and taking turns in the classroom. (Demo Lesson.)	- Tchr sets scene. Refer separate sheet for Groups and Material set out on Work Areas. - Chn work co-operatively to produce a puppet from material supplied. - Tchr to observe and monitor skills being used - To note oral, physical, body language being used by individuals, small grps. - Conclusion - chn to talk about what they found hard, easy, - why they completed, did not complete, puppet. - Share an experience using their puppets

Evaluations O.P.

Kay Greaves.
13. 9. 94.

Figure 1-13. Teacher planning sheet

The children are quick with suggestions:
"What's your favorite color?"
"Do you watch TV?"
"What do you like to eat?"
"Where do you live?"
"Do you collect things?"

"Have you any baby brothers or sisters?"

Kay is delighted: "You'd all make wonderful TV interviewers!"

She now sends the children off in partners. They "find a space" in the room and begin to ask each other questions. The teacher moves about the room, listening, nodding, interacting where she feels it is necessary. There is a buzz of conversation but no loud voices. The atmosphere is busy and intimate. After a few minutes she stops them.

"Thank you, children. That was lovely. We know lots about each other. This morning I introduced our visitor to you, didn't I? Well, now I want you to introduce your partner to the class. If I was introducing Ryan, I might say: Girls and boys, I'd like you to meet Ryan. He has a big sister and a pet cat called Mittens. His favorite color is red and today he is wearing a red shirt!'"

She gives the children a few minutes to practice their introductions, and then she brings them all back onto the rug and one at a time they introduce each other.

The teacher now takes a large piece of paper and clips it onto the easel. "That's one way to let people know about someone else – to tell people about them. If I wanted you to know about Kate I could tell you about her. But I wonder if there is another way we can help other people to get to know her."

The teacher now picks up a crayon and looks at Kate thoughtfully.

"You could draw her!"

"Of course!"

The teacher now points out that she has left large sheets of paper and crayons on their tables. Yes, they're going to draw their partners, too. After a few key instructions, the children are sent back to their tables with their partners and they begin to capture each other on paper. Interestingly enough, the oral "interview" still goes on: while the children draw they also continue to ask questions and talk about themselves. The teacher moves about, discussing, commenting, encouraging.

Some of the children begin to finish their artwork. The teacher stops the children and holds up one of their magnificent portraits.

"What have we done this afternoon? We've introduced our partners to the class by...?

"*Talking* about them!"

"Yes, we've talked about them. Then what did we do?"

"We drew our pictures!"

"Yes, we introduced our partners by *drawing* them. How else could we let people know about them?" The teacher takes a piece of paper cut in the shape of a speech bubble and tapes it to the portrait.

The children respond eagerly: "We could *write* something!"

"Yes. We could write a speech bubble, and then we could have the person telling us something special about themselves. We'll have to have the person's name, too, won't we? If you want to write your own speech bubble, that's fine. And if you want some help, that's fine, too. Just wait 'til I get to you."

So now the children continue with their drawings. The teacher gives out the paper for the drafting and publishing of the speech bubbles and talks to the children as she goes. As they finish their portraits they begin to think about their captions and to try out their ideas. Some are easily able to draft and edit their own. Some need help with some of the words and others tell the teacher what they want her to scribe for them. Kay has left an ample supply of paper for this activity, and the children edit and work through a number of drafts before commencing their final publication copy. Of course, Kay could have also chosen to have the children write in their draft books first, before going on to publish their edited and proofread work in the

The Integration of Learning

New Zealand teachers are very comfortable working with an integrated curriculum. They want children to make connections between what they are studying in one content area with what they are studying or have experienced in another. Science enriches art, art informs social studies, social studies provides challenges for health or music or mathematics, and so on. As for language – it infuses and develops through all curriculum areas.

Note, too, the way the teacher has moved the learning through a range of language modes. The children have talked and listened, have written and read, have drawn (or "presented") and viewed, and have interacted as "whole people" with each other. Not only is the learning integrated but the experiences have been integrated, too.

Lastly, note that the learning has been purposeful. This is not a "practice," or an "exercise," or a "rehearsal" for the real thing. The children appreciate that what they are doing has meaning and purpose and practical validity.

speech bubbles. However, in this case, because of the particular length and presentation requirements of the speech bubble itself, it seemed more helpful to try out the form while also trying out their ideas.

Children who have finished begin to move around the room looking at the other children's portraits and reading the captions to each other. The teacher begins to staple the finished portraits up on the wall. The children eagerly help.

The end of the day is now drawing near. Parents begin to arrive. Some wait outside on the outdoor seating, but others come right into the room. They know they are welcome, but they also know that this is the class work space and they wait respectfully by the door so as not to distract the teacher and the children. While the children are packing up and putting all the crayons and papers away, the teacher goes over and chats with some of the parents. To the mother of a child who started school two days ago she says: "Come and see her picture and the lovely writing she's been doing."

"This is Natalie," the child explains. "She's my friend." The parent smiles and shyly gives her child a hug.

Three o'clock is "home time." The children gather on the rug with their bags. The teacher reminds them about some of the things they have been doing, and they all have a "big think" about the day. She thanks them for their big smiles and dismisses the children individually by name. The parents collect their children and say good-bye. One stops for a brief chat – he just wants to know how his son is settling in. Two children continue to staple up the remaining portraits. The room begins to empty.

And so the day comes to an end for the children. They have discussed, shared experiences, written, drawn, read, listened to poems, talked about books, traded ideas, imagined, reflected, laughed, thought hard, worked on their own, worked with others, have been helped, have helped others... and above all, have grown! Perhaps the most abiding quality in this classroom is the tremendous sense of community. This is a learning community, with a strong sense of family and positive support for everyone. There is a Maori word for this empowering all-embracing concept – *whanau.*

Kay Greaves now looks around her silent room. The day may be over for the children, but not for the teacher. This afternoon after school there is a faculty meeting (or what New Zealand teachers call a "staff meeting") so she only has time for some quick organization – she will have to finish it later. She begins to gather up her notes for the meeting.

Chapter 2

Multicultural Learning: Inside a Junior 1 Classroom

Welcome to Papatoetoe North Primary School

Figure 2-1. Papatoetoe North Primary School

Papatoetoe North Primary School blends into a street of modest bungalows in one of Auckland's residential suburbs. In socioeconomic terms, most families would be lower middle class and below. The majority live in their own homes, with a small number living in rented houses and apartments (or what in New Zealand would be called "flats" and "home units"). A few families "share" an accommodation. Many people living in this area have felt the effects of the current economic recession and there are signs of genuine poverty (relative to the New Zealand setting). However, there is also a strong local pride and the school itself is clearly valued by the community. Classroom presentations and sports days are very well supported by parents, and they also help with the preparation of resource material for teaching, class trips, the school lunch scheme, and in the school library.

The ethnic composition of the school roll is interesting. Fifty percent of the students are Caucasian (including both New Zealand born and those who have recently immigrated). An additional 21 percent are Maori and 10 percent are Samoan. The families that make up the remaining 19 percent are largely from the Pacific Islands and Asian countries. As a result, the school's multicultural diversity gives it a special character. The majority of the children come from two-parent families but a number of families have one parent in sole charge – usually the mother, but not in every case. There are other family compositions, too, such as extended families, "reconstituted" families, families where one parent is a stepparent, and families where the chief caregivers are not the children's birth parents. In fact, this pattern of a mix of family settings would be fairly typical of any New Zealand community now.

School 2: Papatoetoe North Primary School

Location: Inner-city suburban school in a strongly multicultural neighborhood

School Type: A large "contributing primary school" – one that takes children from Junior 1 (age 5) to Standard 4 (about age 10)

Roll: 650 students

Staff: 26, including a principal, deputy principal, assistant principal, and five senior teachers

School Organization: The school is organized on "traditional" New Zealand lines, with twenty single-cell classroom units. Twelve of these rooms, in three blocks of four, are permanent structures, and the remaining eight classrooms are "relocatables." There are two other relocatable buildings – one housing the school library and one a classroom used as a general purpose utility room, or what New Zealand teachers would call a "resource room." The school also has a school hall.

All classes are organized heterogeneously, i.e., there is no attempt to track or stream or group according to ability. The educational programs within the school are based on a developmental philosophy of learning and children's individual interests, needs, and abilities are recognized and catered to. Reading Recovery® is available for children diagnosed as at risk in learning to read and write.

Staff Organization: The staff are organized in teams, with the deputy principal leading the Standard 2 to 4 teachers and the assistant principal leading the New Entrants to Junior 3 classes.

Community Involvement: This is very strong. As an indication, about 90 percent of the parents attend the formal parent-teacher interviews which are held three times a year.

Strong professional leadership and a committed staff have made this a very popular school – so much so that the school has had to introduce an "enrollment scheme." (See page 5 for more information about this.) Many of the classrooms are "relocatables" (see page 38), which is a clear indication of how the school's roll has grown in recent years. A major community fund-raising drive has resulted in the school being able to build its own school hall with full kitchen facilities, which is not only used extensively by the school but by the community as well. Other facilities provided through parent and community fund-raising include a school swimming pool and a resource room and work area for ancillary staff.

The children attending the school live nearby. Most of the children walk to school, although a large number are driven to school by their parents.

The Resource Room

Teachers use the "resource room" for a range of purposes: for music when they need more space than the classroom offers, for theme project work, to leave unfinished projects to dry or spread out ready for further work, or for small groups of children to work on something on their own, e.g., the preparation of a play. Teachers and parent helpers may also use it as a meeting space and a place where teaching resources can be prepared or assembled.

A Day in the Life of Lesley West's Classroom

The time is eight o'clock. It is a warm, clear morning in late autumn. The school grounds are quiet and very still. The brightly colored adventure playground, that is a kind of centerpiece for the school's parklike grounds, is empty. Some children have already arrived at school. Their parents have dropped them off on their way to work. But the school is not officially open until 8:30 A.M. so they sit on the school's outdoor seating, waiting for the bell that will tell them they can enter the classrooms and start the school day.

Meanwhile, Lesley West is busy in her room. Today the class will continue their theme work on tapa cloth, and she checks to make sure she has the materials she needs. She also checks her reading board –

yes, she has the activities and children's names in the right places. She attaches a clean sheet of paper to the easel in the front of the room, ready for today's shared story. She also checks the Beginning School Mathematics equipment – yes, the children put everything away in the right place yesterday...

The Class

Class Level: J1 (Junior 1)
Teacher: Lesley West
School: Papatoetoe North Primary School
Equivalent U.S. Grades: Grade 1
Years Students Have Spent at School: 1 to 2 years
Ages: 5 years, 7 months to 6 years, 4 months
Number of Children in the Class: 29
Student Composition:

Ethnicity	*First Language*
12 New Zealand European	English
7 part Maori	English
3 part Samoan	Samoan and English
3 Taiwanese	Chinese
1 part Tongan	Tongan and English
1 West Indian	English and Hindi
1 from Cook Islands	English
1 Vietnamese	Vietnamese

The Room

Lesley West's classroom is a "relocatable." It has its own entry porch and there are windows on both sides of the room so natural light floods in throughout the day. It has electric heaters for use in winter. (Auckland's winters are mild. There may be the odd frosty morning, but generally the temperature is around 40 to 50 degrees Fahrenheit, so an electric heater is all that is needed to keep the space warm.)

The room is full to overflowing with learning centers, resource ideas, displays, samples of children's work, art and craft activities in progress, ongoing science experiments, book displays, reading corners, and, of course, one teacher and very soon the 29 children who live and work here each day! Space is at a premium and the teacher had to plan the use of the room with great care to ensure flexibility and movement.

Figure 2-2. Lesley West's classroom

Sitting in this classroom, one can't help but interact with the materials. Up front is a life-size body with all its parts labeled in Maori. There are also charts that give the Maori names for numbers, days of the week, and colors. Although English is the main language of instruction in the classroom, throughout the day the teacher will use words and phrases in Maori and the children are free to respond in whatever language they feel confident with.

In the front of the room is a blackboard on which Lesley has written a message to the class, outlining the plan for the day.

Today's Program

Fitness
Writing
Playtime
SSR
Reading
Lunch
Poems
Math
Art/Social Studies
Story
Home Time

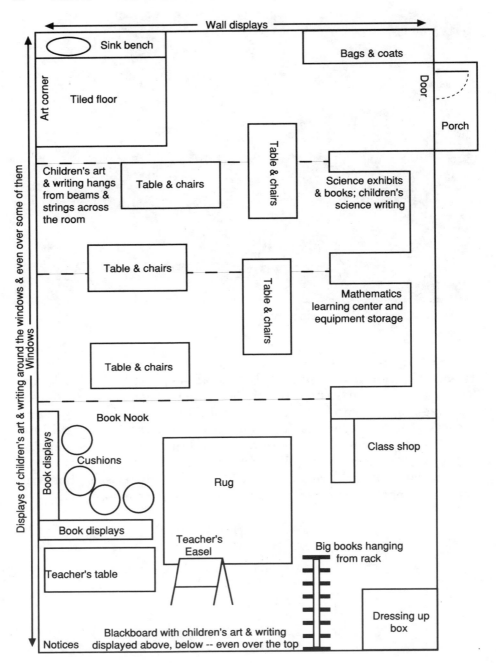

Figure 2-3. Diagram of Lesley West's Classroom

Learning Centers

U.S. teachers often use the term "learning center" to describe a display or resource that has been carefully structured to bring about quite specific and predictable learning. Sometimes New Zealand teachers use the term in this way too, but they are more likely to describe any area of their classroom where stimulating resources are available to the children as a "learning center." The interaction is not prescribed or specific and the possible outcomes are many and varied. Such a "learning center" could be a collection of books on a topic or theme, a box of teacher- and student-made poetry cards, a giant wall story painted by the children depicting events in a favorite story, a dressing-up box, a classroom shop with plastic money and empty packets from the supermarket, or some interactive posters with activity suggestions and some available reference materials to assist with the activities. It could also be some kind of interactive "environment" such as a puppet theater, the inside of a giant papier-mâché volcano (made by the children!) where the children as exploring vulcanologists can write about and draw their scientific discoveries and hypotheses, or an historical school desk that the children can sit at and read, listen to tapes, and think about what school was like 50 years ago. (All these are examples of "learning centers" observed recently in New Zealand classrooms.)

Above the blackboard is a colorful display of life-size paper "T-shirts" – one for each child in the class and each featuring a color photo of the child and a positive comment. "Anthony plays well with other people." "Al-roy helps people who have difficulties." "Aroha is a kind helper."

Along one side of the room there is a dressing-up box, and a sign invites children to do a little dressing up if they wish. There is also a classroom shop which sells a range of (empty) household packages and containers. There is a mathematics storage area and a science corner. On the other side of the room there is the teacher's desk, the class library, and samples of the children's published writing, including a magnificent wall story based on the children's own retelling of *Greedy Cat* (Cowley 1983).

It's now 8:30 A.M. and the school bell rings. The early children hurry into the classroom eagerly. They greet their teacher. Some have special things they are just bursting to tell her. The teacher needs helpers for tasks, too. They hang up their schoolbags in the cloak-room, assist the teacher, and then make their way outside to play.

Typical Daily Schedule

9:00 – 9:10	Fitness
9:10 – 10:30	Language: oral sharing, shared writing, independent writing
10:30 – 10:45	Break
10:45 – 12:00	Language continues: shared reading, independent reading, and other reading/writing activities
12:00 – 1:00	Lunch and Break
1:00 – 1:30	Mathematics
1:30 – 3:00	Theme (Language/Art/Social Studies/Science/Health)

Nine o'clock and the bell sounds for the start of the day. In Lesley West's room the routines are familiar. Before entering the room, the teacher leads the children through some vigorous fitness exercises. They do their own version of aerobics to taped music, followed by some quick vigorous relay games. Ten minutes later they file into the classroom where they make their way straight to the mat.

Lesley West sits on her low teacher's chair and smiles at her five-and six-year-olds: "Tena koutou Ruma Rua Tekau. I hope you are all kei te pai today." (Greetings, Room Twenty. I hope you are all feeling pretty good today.)

The children grin back and reply in their characteristic drawn-out sing-song way, "Kia ora, Ms. West." They are all seated on the mat in front of her, all 29 of them, each one hugging their knees and clearly eager to start the day.

First the attendance register has to be marked:

"Kia ora, Matthew."

"Kia ora, Ms. West."

"Konichiwa, Daniel."

"Konichiwa, Ms. West."

"Good morning, Sofia."

"Good morning, Ms. West..."

Every morning the children have an opportunity to share their news with the rest of the class. Today the teacher has something special to tell the children, too. "In our afternoon theme time we've been

Fitness

New Zealand schools do not have gymnasiums or physical education specialists. Instead, this area of the curriculum (along with every other area of the primary school curriculum) is the responsibility of the classroom teacher. Fitness is conducted regularly – usually daily – and is enjoyed by the children and the teacher. Thanks to the mild winters and pleasant summers, the stereotypical "New Zealand lifestyle" has a strong "outdoors" orientation, with many New Zealanders taking part in a wide range of sporting and recreational pursuits.

thinking and talking about tapa cloth lately, haven't we?" The children nod eagerly. Many of the children in this class are from families from the Pacific Islands and they already know a great deal about how this traditional cloth is made. "I was talking to Mrs. Sharp about tapa cloth yesterday and she gave me this lovely book to show you." She shows the children some of the photographs in the book and reads a little about how tapa cloth is made.

"'After the bark has been scraped and beaten...'" she reads, then stops to reflect. "Scraped... what other things get scraped?"

"You scrape potatoes."

"You can scrape vegetables, too."

"An orange."

"Like when you scrape your knee."

The teacher listens and nods thoughtfully to each suggestion, then she reads on. "It is then decorated with patterns...' What's a pattern? I wonder if anyone is wearing something with a pattern on it.

Greetings from a Range of Cultures

One way New Zealand teachers recognize and express value for other languages and cultures is to acknowledge them through the use of greetings and other language rituals. The learning is incidental and subtle, but perhaps all the more valuable because of it.

Asia stands up to show the flowery pattern on her dress (a "frock" to New Zealanders). Avril has black and white dots on her clothes. Mary has green and white stripes.

"And now the book says these patterns come from the 'natural environment.' That is a hard concept. The natural environment. I wonder if anyone can help us with this one. Have a think about it first of all."

The children all have "a think." No one is very sure what it could mean. Mary is prepared to try out an idea, though. "Is it like water and trees and stuff?"

The teacher nods thoughtfully. "I think Mary is helping us think along the right lines. Perhaps I can explain it like this. Where would you expect to find a fish living?"

"In the water."

"The river."

"The sea."

"Right. And those would be the fish's natural environment. And where would you expect to find a bird living?"

"In a tree."

"What about a person? What about a child? Would a child live in the water?"

The Book as an Information Resource

The teacher has introduced the book to the class very carefully. The text may well be too difficult for most of the children to read but the illustrations are very accessible and highly relevant to the theme topic, hence her emphasis. Note the way she has modeled the use of a reference resource like this – flipping through the pages, selecting passages to read in detail, and using the contents page and index for further research.

The book remains "on display" and available for the children to refer to in their own time – and throughout the next few days, most of the children will spend some time browsing through its pages and looking at the designs in particular. In this way it will inform their own art projects and enrich their understandings of the lives and cultures of the peoples of the Pacific.

Clothespins to Hold Everything Up!

In New Zealand clothespins are called clothes *pegs*. In fact, clothes pegs are used extensively by New Zealand teachers for attaching just about everything in the classroom. It's one of those innovative little ideas that some teacher discovered worked well and shared with the teacher in the room next door and so the idea got around. Sometimes the best teacher in-service is what you learn from the teacher in the next room!

"No!" say the children.

"Would a child live in a tree?"

"No!" say the children again, but one child is not so hasty: "They might if it was in a tree hut!"

Lesley laughs. "When we talk about the 'natural environment' we're talking about where things normally are, or where they like to be, or where you usually find them. So if the patterns came from the natural environment, it means they found the patterns all about them where they lived. There are some lovely pictures of the patterns in this book and also photos of where the people live so you can see where the patterns came from. I'm going to leave them out so you can have a look at them before we do our own tapa cloth patterns this afternoon.

"But now it is time to write our class story." Every morning the teacher writes a shared story with the children. She writes on a large piece of paper pinned to a small easel with clothespins.

Today Lesley chooses to write about the tapa cloth ideas they are working on. She speaks her thoughts out loud as she writes. It is all part of the modeling process. Also, pinned to her easel is the same alphabet sheet all the children have beside them when they are writing. Each letter has a drawing of something that starts with that letter and the children use it to help prompt them with the letter sounds.

"I am so excited about the tapa cloth we're going to make that I want to write about it today. Now, how shall I begin?"

"Don't forget to start with a capital letter," prompts Sofia.

"Thank you." And the teacher begins writing while speaking, "'I... was... on... my... way... to... school... this... morning...' morn – *ing*.

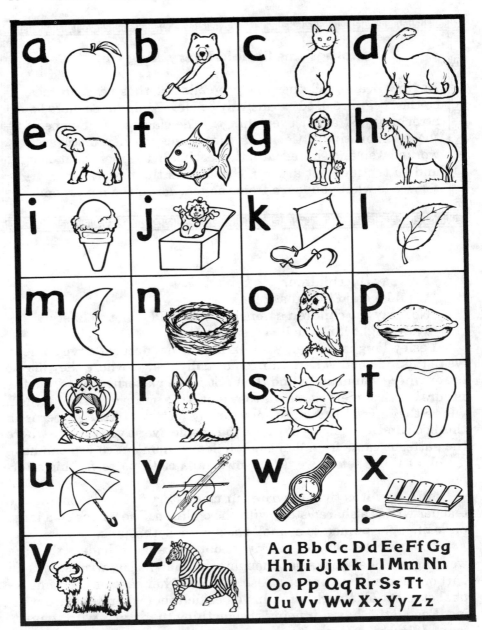

Figure 2-4. Alphabet Card

What does *morning* end with?" Eager helpers put up their hands:

"i-n-g!" says Brad.

"It ends the same way as swimming," Melissa volunteers.

"And how does *morning* start?" asks the teacher, picking up her alphabet sheet.

"It starts like my name!" says Michael, all smiles.

"Good!" the teacher declares and gets ready to continue writing. First, however, she reminds herself of a good strategy. "What was that good idea we had the other day? Oh yes, I must read it all again so I remember what I have written so far." By thinking aloud like this the teacher is helping the children rehearse valuable writing strategies. They not only see what she does but they hear her say what she is doing. In this way they are learning not only the writing process but they are also learning to verbalize about it.

"'I was on my way to school this morning and... I... was... thinking... about...' *About* looks funny to me. I'm not sure if I have spelled that correctly or not. I don't really want to stop writing now because I want to keep my ideas going. I don't want to forget what it is I want to say."

Rowan knows what to do. "Put a line under it to remind you to check it later."

"Of course! Thank you, Rowan." The teacher continues writing, "'...thinking about... our... tapa... cloth... and... I... decided...' How does *decided* end?"

And so the activity goes on. The teacher and the children finish their shared story and it remains on the easel for all to read. Sometimes the class will decide to "publish" the story and turn it into a big book for everyone to read. When this happens, all the children will help illustrate it. They may even write pieces for it. But for now, today's story remains on the easel – a reminder that in this class everyone is a writer – the children and the teacher, and they all help each other.

After this group "warm-up," it is now the children's turn to do their own independent writing. All the children write every day, but to ensure that all children work some pieces through to publication, the teacher has a writing task board and lists the children who should be working on the publication phase of one of their pieces. The task board also suggests optional activities for children who have completed their writing.

Lesley comments, "I was so pleased with Jessy's story from yesterday. Look, she's putting full stops in!" (In New Zealand, periods are referred to as "full stops" – maybe because that's what you do when

Writing Today

Publishing Today:
Gus, Micah, Azure, Amy, David G., Michael, Nathan, Teresa, Sanoh, Jessy, Anthony

Options for writers who have finished:
ABC alphabet, computer, play dough, drawing / illustrating, listening post, science table, publishing, flower construction, spelling practice, handwriting practice, building blocks.

Figure 2-5. Writing Task Board

you're reading?) "That's lovely, Jessy! You've shown me where to stop when I am reading and think about what you have said. And look, Jessy is putting lines under the words she is not sure about, too! Well done, Jessy! Aroha, I'd like you to work with me today. Amy and Sanoh, I'd like you to buddy read before starting your stories. Brad and George, I'd like you to buddy read, too, before starting your publishing. Same for Matthew and Nathan."

The teacher now sends the children off with their books. The writers sit at the tables, take up their pencils, and immediately are involved in their writing. Alongside they keep their alphabet chart handy in case they are unsure of a letter sound or how to form a particular letter. Lesley begins to rove and conference with individual children as she goes.

The children are writing on a great variety of topics. Rowan is writing about a visit to a museum. Micah is writing about going to the "picture theatre" (what U.S. readers would call the movies).

Buddy Reading

"Buddy reading" in writing, which teachers sometimes refer to as a revising conference, may involve the writer reading to another child who then acts as the audience or reader, or it may involve another child reading back a piece of writing to its writer. Both procedures are helpful, although the former is the more usual. Children can be "buddied" with a child of similar ability, or with a child who is more or less capable – it all depends on the teacher's purpose, and that is why it is usual for the teacher to choose the children's partners. As the purpose changes, so the children chosen to be buddies will change.

Having to read one's own piece often makes the writer "hear it for themselves." In order to "make sense of it" for their audience, they are encouraged to critically appraise what they have written, and frequently children will make spontaneous corrections and improvements while they are reading. The listening child will also follow the text and is encouraged to give feedback on the writing. This may be about specific textural features, such as spelling and punctuation, but it is also helpful if the receiving child responds to the writer's ideas or meaning or the mood of the piece.

Children need to be taught how to do this. The teacher needs to model this and may also give children good "comment starters" to help them respond to each other's work, such as: "I like the way... When you read that I was feeling... The best part for me was... That made me think about...I heard you say... You said..."

Buddy reading is also valuable because it clearly demonstrates one of the key reasons we write – to communicate our ideas and to share our feelings and experiences. The classroom writing becomes *real* writing, not practice writing for the time when they will need to do the real thing.

Writing Conferences[1]

Writing conferences can serve a whole range of purposes: they can help stimulate ideas, solve problems, sharpen the writer's focus on meaning and intention, assist with editing and proof-reading, encourage collaboration, provide motivation, support risk-taking, discuss publication, set deadlines, and help develop a sense that this is a community of writers.

Writing conferences may be
- **Individual** – when the teacher works one-on-one with a child to help with some aspect of either the composition phase of writing (clarifying ideas, choice of topic, choice of genre, choice of voice, prewriting planning, drafting, and editing) or with the preparation for publication phase of writing (proofreading, spelling skills, punctuation skills, presentation skills, and design ideas).
- **Roving** – when the teacher makes short calls on each child, finding out what they are writing about, where they are in their draft, and whether they need any help at that point.
- **Partner** – when children get together in pairs (or "buddies") to tell each other about their writing or comment on each other's writing, or listen to each other reading a passage from their work, or talking about what they have discovered or learned about their own writing and the writing process.
- **Group** – when a group of writers meets to share and discuss their drafts. Writers may call a group conference because they need help to solve a particular problem in their writing or want a wider audience to share their work and discoveries with more children than just a partner.

---

[1] For more information on writing conferences, see Ministry of Education. 1992. *Dancing with the Pen: The Learner as a Writer*. Wellington, New Zealand: Learning Media, pp 104–108.

Sarah's piece is about her aunty. The buddy readers help each other quietly and then begin their own writing. Lesley roves, conferencing with individual children and helping them with strategies to assist them to become independent writers. She also carries her own monitoring book with her and notes observations about individual children's writing as she sees significant changes. Sometimes the children prompt her with their discoveries about their writing, too. Chris shows her how he has set out the title to his piece, and she responds, "That's lovely, Chris. You used capital letters in your title. I'm so pleased. I'm going to make a note of that in my book."

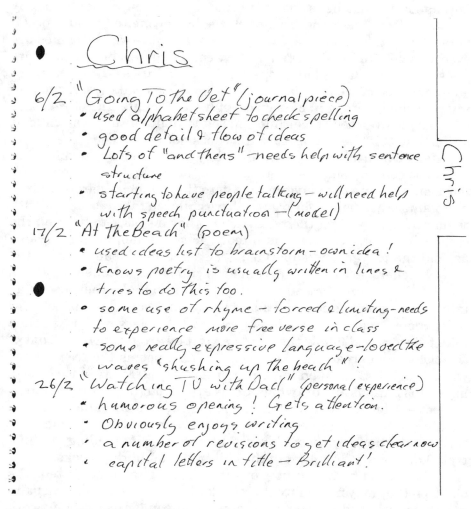

Figure 2-6. Teacher's Notebook Entry

It is now 10:25 A.M. and the children begin to pack up their writing things. Those who have finished now get out their chosen reading books so they will be ready for independent reading when they come back into the class after the break. Then they gather on the mat.

"David finished publishing his story this morning and I think it is very interesting. He really made me think when I read it, and he described what happened so well that when I read it, it was as if I was there and I could see it too." She begins to read and the children listen intently. At 10:30 A.M. the bell sounds.

"I think we're all ready to go to play. Today is Micah's Special Day so I'm going to let her choose the groups that are ready." Micah now sits in the teacher's chair and chooses the groups that are ready for play. Every week the teacher chooses someone to be her "special person" and this week it is Micah's turn. It is one way to make sure everyone gets to be "famous for the week." The teacher makes sure the special person has lots of special responsibilities during the week – but she also makes a point of observing the special person and seeing how she is coping in all aspects of her school life. In a large class it is easy to overlook some children, so by "highlighting" one child at a time like this she makes sure that does not happen.

As Micah dismisses the children they make their way to the cloakroom and collect a snack – what they call their "playlunch" – and then move outside into the playground where they munch their food, chat, or organize themselves for a game. Two children take a book out with them and after eating their playlunch, they sit back-to-back on the outside seating, reading contentedly. The teacher on duty walks around the playground supervising the children. Meanwhile all the other teachers go to the staffroom for a cup of tea or coffee.

10:45 A.M. and the bell rings. The children make their own way into the classroom and immediately take out their chosen books for independent reading. Some, in pairs, read the class big books. They take pointers and follow the words as if they are teachers in front of the class. Some read the class poem cards – poems the teacher has written in felt-tip pen on large poster-size cards. Many of these also have illustrations and drawings. Some are cut out in the shape of their subject – a butterfly card, a frog-shaped card, a card shaped like a wishing well. All have been made by the teacher, although some feature illustrations by the children. Al-roy is happily reading an illustrated dictionary, but most of the children read library books.

After about eight minutes of silent reading the teacher tells the children they may now share their books. The children buddy, in pairs mostly. Some read to their partners. Some ponder over the artwork and comment on the illustrations. Lesley, too, sits with the children to do some "book talk." One boy in this group has been reading a *National Geographic* and he and the teacher talk about the quality of the photographs. Some of the children now begin to "read the room" – that is, they move about the room reading the text they find as they go – children's stories, captions for science exhibits, questions to guide social studies observations, children's poems, and so on.

It is now 11:00 A.M. The teacher sings to the children to "put their books away and come to the mat." As they gather she sings quietly and the children join in happily. When everyone is ready, she puts her guitar down and picks up a poem card. It is one of their favorites: "Jump or Jiggle." They all read it together, and then they try it with actions:

> *"Frogs jump, caterpillars hump,*
> *Worms wiggle, bugs jiggle,*
> *Rabbits hop, horses clop..."*

(Beyer in Mitchell 1937)

One of the children has a bright idea. "We should do this poem for fitness!"

The teacher thinks that's an excellent idea. "You must remind me tomorrow when we're doing fitness, Al-roy."

Now it is time for shared reading. She has chosen "When the King Rides By" by Margaret Mahy (1986a).

> *"Oh what a fuss when the King rides by.*
> *The pussy-cat runs and the pigeons fly*
> *And the drum goes rat-a-tat-tat..."*

The text is on display and the children join in the reading with relish. It is a story that builds up a pattern. One child is chosen to be the drummer and do the "rat-a-tat-tats." When they reach the end, the children want it all over again. This time, the teacher stops now and then to "notice" things in the text. She finds an exclamation mark (or point). Matthew points out a "line in the middle of 'pussy-cat'." The teacher explains that it joins the two words together and that it is called a "hyphen." Al-roy's eyes light up. He rushes to the reading board to point out that his name has a hyphen in it, too!

11:30 A.M. and it is now time for the class's individualized reading program. The children's names are on a magnetic notice board and alongside are lists of activities the teacher wants them to do today. One group is to go to the listening posts and listen to a story while they follow it in the text. Two groups have book boxes – selected books that are appropriate for their level of reading – emergent, early or nearly fluent, and fluent. One group will work with word jigsaws. Some children are to read to each other in pairs, and some are to read the big books or to read around the room. One group has "free choice." Another group works with the teacher. No explanations are needed – the children just move off and start work on the appropriate task.

The children work at their activities. The teacher moves on to another group. At about 11:55 A.M., she tells the class to pack up, and the children immediately begin to put their things away. All jigsaws and word activity kits are carefully stored in plastic bags. Library books go back to the classroom library. As the children clear their areas, they gather on the mat. The teacher asks Micah to choose children who are ready to go to lunch and gradually the class is dismissed.

They collect their lunches from their school bags, and they sit on the seats and the concrete outside the classroom to eat their lunch. The duty teacher moves among them, chatting, supervising, laughing at a child's joke here, answering a serious question there. The children munch their lunches – mostly bread sandwiches with a range of fillings – and chat, laugh, listen, eat... The teachers make their way to the staffroom where they all eat together too – and chat, laugh, listen, eat...

Lunch is from noon to 1 o'clock in this school. At 1 o'clock the bell rings again and the children make their way into the classroom. It is now time for mathematics. Organization for the lesson is set out on the magnetic board. The teacher quickly marks the attendance register for the afternoon and then sets the children to work. As with the reading activities, the teacher expects the children to be able to see what they are supposed to do and to begin themselves. The mathematics center is taken up with shelves of plastic containers (used ice-cream containers the children have brought from home). There are sets of commercial mathematics equipment, such as colored rods, a variety of building and interlocking blocks, and so on, but there are also lots of "found" materials – bottle tops, plastic milk carton caps, beads, film containers, walnut shells, wheels, pebbles, shells, and the like.

Today Lesley begins with the Squares. They work with the colored rods first, making and then developing patterns and discussing

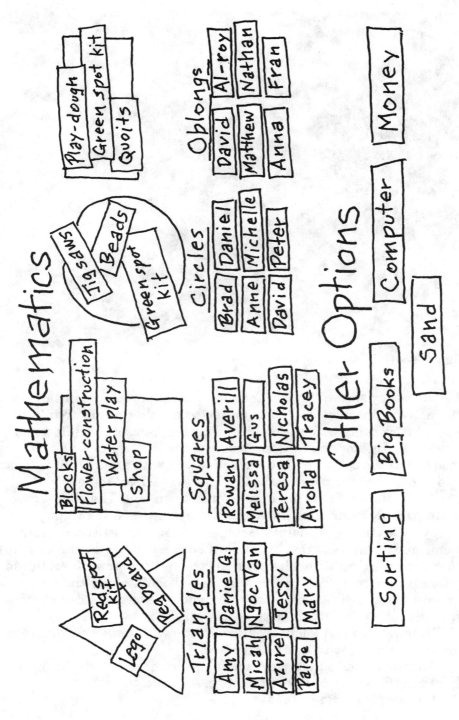

Figure 2-7. Mathematics

Figure 2-8. Children doing math

the ideas they show. The teacher shows them how they can carry on
this activity in pairs and then moves to another group. While the
teacher is working with the children in groups, the other children are
independently working at their assigned tasks. They talk when they
need to, but the children have learned to talk with a voice that is "just
loud enough for the person who is supposed to hear, to hear."

1:30 P.M. and math time now comes to an end. The children begin to pack up their equipment and store it away in the right place.
Lesley is getting the materials together for the art/social studies
theme activity for the rest of the day, so she calls on Micah to help
"look after the class." Micah sits on the teacher's chair as the children
gather on the mat. The groups that have been making things have
brought along their creations to share with the class. Micah chooses
them one at a time to talk to the class.

Brad has a play-dough creature to show. "I made this dinosaur
and it has an egg with it. Any questions?"

Amy has made a pattern. "I made this in the shape of a heart and
there are strawberries round the edge. Any questions?"

Rowan: "How did you make it?"

Amy: "I used a play-dough knife for the outside and I made the strawberry pattern with my fingernails."

It is now 1:40 P.M. The teacher thanks Micah and holds up the book she showed the class at the start of day.

"Can you remember what we were talking about this morning?"

"Tapa cloth."

"Making dyes."

"The natural environment!"

The teacher is surprised. "You remembered that, too? I'm very impressed! We talked about bark, too, didn't we? And guess what Brad and Matthew found during the lunchtime?"

"Some bark!"

"Yes! They've put it on the science table and they've written a card telling us all where they found it and what kind of tree they think it came from."

Lesley then shows them tapa cloth patterns in the book. Some of these she has copied onto big sheets of paper, and she now holds them up for the children to look at.

"Remember, we said they often used patterns from the natural environment. Where do you think these patterns may have come from?"

The children have no trouble making connections: "Spiders webs."

"Flowers."

"Leaves."

There are some odd ideas, too. Matthew says it reminds him of wallpaper!

"That's interesting," says the teacher. "I'll have to think about that."

Lesley then shows how she used a large crayon to make the pattern. She practices on a piece of newspaper first. When she is happy with the pattern, she begins to draw it on one of the panels. The children watch intently. Soon it is their turn. The teacher chooses some helpers to spread newspaper on the tables, and when all is ready, the children quickly collect their sheets of art paper and begin to experiment with their own patterns.

For the rest of the afternoon the children refine their patterns and begin to finalize the designs they will use on their own tapa cloths. As they work, the teacher moves about, talking about the children's creations as she goes. She discusses their choice of color, the way the pattern will need to contrast textures, and the natural objects they have chosen for their patterns. She asks them to think about the Pacific Islands where tapa cloth comes from, too. This is art, social studies, and language all interwoven. The children talk quietly as they work and as their patterns are completed, they fasten them with clothespins to a string hanging across the room.

At 2:55 P.M., the teacher asks the children to pack up. The crayons go back in the containers, the newspaper is folded up, and the children gather on the mat. The teacher begins to sing and the children join in.

"I've had a good day today. I wonder if anyone else has had a good day today?" Micah's hand goes up fast! Everyone else puts up their hands, too. "That's wonderful! We've all had a good day. Let's think back over all the things we've done today." The teacher refers to the plan for the day and quickly reviews the day's highlights.

The bell rings. It is three o'clock. The children are dismissed. They gather their bags from the cloakroom and set out for home. The teacher from the next classroom puts her head around the door.

"How did it go?" Another teacher joins them. They have planned this Pacific Island study together and so each is keen to know how it is developing in the different classrooms. One class has mastered a song from Tonga, and the teacher offers to let some of her children come and teach the children in the other classrooms: not only do the children "work collaboratively," but the teachers do, too!

Chapter 3

Language Across the Curriculum:
Inside a Junior 2 and 3 Classroom

Welcome to Bayview Primary School

Figure 3-1. Bayview Primary School

Bayview Primary School is on the fringe of the city of Auckland, where town meets country. It nestles into a gully that runs on down to the sea. Modest suburban houses cling to the hillsides among clumps of tree fern and native bush. Adjoining the school grounds is the Bayview Community Center, a hall which the school uses during the day and which is shared with all the local community clubs and social groups.

Also alongside the school is the Bayview Free Kindergarten, a preschool center for children aged three to five. There is continual liaison between the school and the kindergarten. Once a month the kindergarten head teacher meets with the school principal and the junior class teachers. In addition, the kindergarten children are invited to participate in some of the school's regular weekly assemblies and sharing sessions.

Like most New Zealand schools, Bayview Primary School's classrooms are all on the ground floor. Each room opens out onto concrete courtyards where children can play during breaks and where they can sit to eat their lunches throughout the year (except on wet days, when they eat their lunches inside the classroom). The larger expanses of concrete may also be used for class fitness. In the front of the school there are concrete courts where the children may choose to play "patter-tennis" – a kind of tennis using a smaller court and played with a wooden paddle instead of a conventionally strung racket. The school also has a large grass field which is used for physical education, sports (such as athletics, football, and softball), and also as a play area by the children during the breaks.

School 3: Bayview Primary School

Location: City suburb
School Type: A "contributing primary school" – one that takes children from Junior 1/New Entrants (age five) to Standard 4 (about age ten)
Roll: 330 students
Staff: Principal, deputy principal (responsible for senior classes, Standard 2 – 4), assistant principal (responsible for the junior classes, New Entrants to Junior 3), and ten class teachers
School Organization: The children are organized into ten classes, three of which are single-grade classes and seven of which are multi-age classes (or "composites").
Staff Organization: All teachers belong to one of two teams or "syndicates" – the junior syndicate (New Entrants to Junior 3) or the senior syndicate (Standards 2 – 4). Syndicate meetings are held weekly, every Monday afternoon. Teachers work together in these to share ideas and to jointly plan the teaching program. Teachers also belong to up to (but not more than) two of the school's five "Curriculum Teams." The five are:

♦ The arts (includes art, music, technology, Maori, other languages, and English for speakers of other languages)

- Mathematics
- Language (includes oral language: speaking and listening; written language: reading and writing; visual language: presenting and viewing; and body language: demonstrating and watching)
- Inquiry studies (includes science and social studies)
- Health and physical well-being

Teacher Commitments: Every second Tuesday there is a full staff meeting after school (3:00 – 5:00 P.M.) for all staff. On every other Tuesday this time is available for curriculum meetings. Syndicate meetings are held every Monday after school (3:00 – 5:00 P.M.). The Senior Management Team (principal, deputy principal and assistant principal) meet every Monday morning before school, and on Wednesday after school.

Parents are encouraged to participate in the life of the school and although in many households both parents or caregivers are working, a significant number still manage to lend a hand as "parent helpers," either in the daily classroom activities or on special events such as class trips. Parents are invited and encouraged to attend the regular Friday school assembly and sharing session, and in fact, many do. The school also provides a language experience and enrichment program for junior class children in need of additional language help and support. This involves one-on-one tutoring from volunteer parents who are trained by the school. It is called the BELL (Bayview Early Language Learning) program, and is coordinated by the New Entrant teachers.

Parents also assist with road-crossing supervision before and after school, but in fact, as with most school pedestrian crossings throughout the country, it is the *children* who actually patrol the crossing – a practice that often startles visiting U.S. teachers! To make them visible to motorists, the children wear brightly colored tunics and hold out signs on poles to stop the traffic when children wish to cross. The children are always from the senior classes – in the case of Bayview Primary School this means they will be ten- or eleven-year-olds – and they receive special training from visiting traffic police officers. Usually they will be supervised by a teacher or volunteer parent, but nonetheless, they will be in charge and taking responsibility for the safety of the children crossing the road. In fact, the scheme works very well, and it is an indication of how much responsibility children can take if we are prepared to trust them.

Recently the school asked the parents and the teachers to participate in a "School Needs Analysis" (see the questionnaire on page 64).

This was prepared and facilitated by Anne Bradstreet (the teacher we are about to meet) as part of her postgraduate teacher studies. Parents were very cooperative – 215 families were surveyed and 175 responded, which is a return rate of 81.4 percent. The responses were very positive and supportive and, in fact, there was only one negative response!

Bayview School Needs Questionnaire[1]

1. What do you think Bayview School should provide for your children?

	Very Important							Unimportant		
– a balanced education	10	9	8	7	6	5	4	3	2	1
– overall happiness	10	9	8	7	6	5	4	3	2	1
– good self-esteem	10	9	8	7	6	5	4	3	2	1
– high academic achievement	10	9	8	7	6	5	4	3	2	1
– good working habits	10	9	8	7	6	5	4	3	2	1
– love of learning	10	9	8	7	6	5	4	3	2	1
– have special needs met	10	9	8	7	6	5	4	3	2	1
– treated as individuals	10	9	8	7	6	5	4	3	2	1
– strong in the "basics"	10	9	8	7	6	5	4	3	2	1
– cultural awareness/sensitivity to others	10	9	8	7	6	5	4	3	2	1
– any other	10	9	8	7	6	5	4	3	2	1

2. What do you think are the three most important?

    1. _____
    2. _____
    3. _____

3. What are the school's main strengths?

    1. _____
    2. _____
    3. _____

4. In what ways is our school special or different from other schools?

    _____
    _____

---

[1] Copyright 1995 Instructional Leadership Conference, Auckland College of Education. Reproduced by permission.

5. If you could change three things in our school, what would you change and how?

1. _____

2. _____

3. _____

6. Any other suggestions/comments?

_____

_____

_____

The staff also completed the same questionnaire and in the section which asked people to list the three most important things the school should be providing for the children, both groups came up with similar choices. Both parents and staff opted for "good self-esteem" and "a balanced education" as their first choices. The staff placed "love of learning" as their third choice, and while the parents ranked this highly, their third choice was "good working habits." Both parents and staff agreed that Bayview was a good school with a strong staff providing balanced programs and good strategies for managing children. A strong sense of community involvement was also endorsed. Both groups highlighted the need for development in the areas of technology, parent education, and communication systems. Staff particularly identified the need for time management. Information from the survey is now being used by the school and its managing Board of Trustees to develop the school's Five-Year School Development Plan.

Welcome to Anne Bradstreet's Classroom

Anne Bradstreet's classroom declares itself loudly as a children's "learning laboratory!" There is evidence of that learning everywhere. An overwhelming array of children's stories, posters, captions, wall stories, murals, displays, exhibits, big books, concertina books, paintings, and artwork cover the walls. Large paintings hang from strings across the room, and adults have to duck beneath them in order to move from one side to the other. There are graphs showing how many cats, dogs, rabbits, horses, and fish the children have at home. There are collages on health education themes; one cluster of children's work declares: "We Love Our Hearts!" There are colorful books on display in the class library corner and learning resource centers displaying a wide range of the children's own work. There are even beautiful paintings pinned flat onto the ceiling!

The Class

Class Level: J2 and J3 (Junior 2 and 3)
Teacher: Anne Bradstreet
School: Bayview Primary School
Equivalent U.S. Grades: Grades 1 and 2
Years Students Have Spent at School: $1\frac{1}{2}$ to $2\frac{1}{2}$ years
Ages: 6 years, 6 months to 7 years, 6 months
Number of Children in the Class: 35
Student Composition:

Ethnicity	*First Language*
30 New Zealand European	English
3 part Maori	English
1 part Tongan	Tongan and English
1 from Germany	German and English

The classroom is built on two levels. The lower level forms the foot of an "L" that flows into the next class's space. The rooms have been built for "open plan" or "variable space" teaching, and while for much of the day the adjoining classes function independently as class units, there are times when the classes do come together to take part in shared activities.

The day begins with twenty minutes of "Fitness." The class moves outside to the field behind the school. Here a number of other classes are collecting, too. Sometimes they combine for fitness, but this morning each class is working with its own teacher. The teacher not only demonstrates and instructs the children, but she also takes part in the activities. (It's a chance for a little "teacher fitness," too!)

They begin with some stretching and warm-up activities. The children all know why they are doing this: currently there is a national campaign to encourage everyone to remember to "extend" before you "stand, stretch, lift, or bend" so as to reduce the high number of back injuries in New Zealand. This is followed by more vigorous activities, including running, team games, some hoop work, jumping rope (what New Zealand children call "skipping"), and culminating in some very active team relay games. The teacher then leads them with "warming down" exercises and they file back into the classroom ready for the day's "school" work.

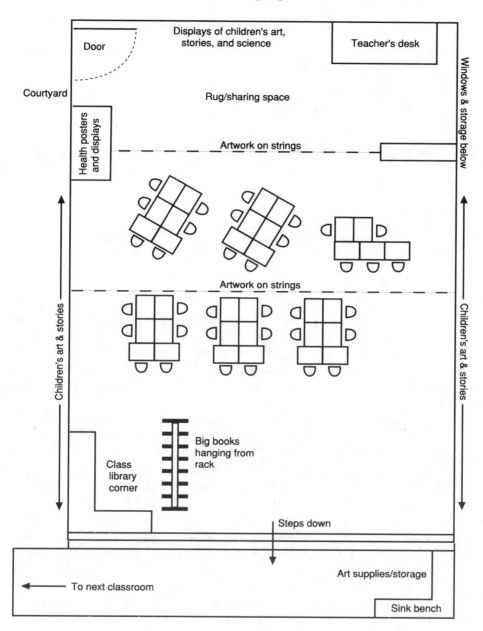

Figure 3-2. Diagram of Anne Bradstreet's Classroom

Typical Daily Schedule

8:30 – 10:45	Fitness, Language (oral discussion, reading, writing)
10:30 – 10:45	Break
10:45 – 11:30	Language continued
11:30 – 12:00	Mathematics
12:00 – 1:00	Lunch and Break
1:00 – 1:15	Reading (independent)
1:15 – 3:00	Theme (Social Studies/Health Education/Science/Technology)

Variations:

Periods of: Physical Education
Music Assembly
School Assembly
Library
Art

First, they gather on the mat for a discussion period. Many of the children have news to share. One has a birthday party to tell about. Another talks about a family event. Throughout, the teacher models good listening. She asks questions for further information and thanks each child for his or her contribution. The children are encouraged to do this, too.

Anne now puts on a glove puppet and begins a dialogue with the children as the puppet character, "Ali." Ali is really an alligator but he's heard all the stories about dragons the teacher has been sharing with the children and has decided he would like to be a dragon, too. This is his "goal," but how is he going to achieve his goal? He needs help from the children.

In fact, goal setting is the class "theme" at the moment. It is part of a social studies topic related to the syllabus question: *Why do people think, feel, and act the way they do when trying to achieve a goal?* But this is an integrated learning program so while the schedule calls this language time, content material from the social studies program is interwoven throughout the language work and, in fact, because of the theme, throughout the whole day.

Anne has also interwoven the work on this theme with a dragon project. This will form the basis for her afternoon theme work and the following are her notes for this.

Figure 3-3. Ali talks to Anne's class

Strange Creatures/Dragons/Dragon World

The Project: The children will create an imaginative creature (dragon or other) in both art form and writing by experiencing a variety of activities. The project will integrate aspects of a number of creative arts.

Sources of Motivation: Stories, poems, music, puppetry, personal experiences, cultural experiences. Narrative introduction: Ali decides to become a dragon – he went to the movies and decided the fantasy world is far more exciting than living in a swamp. What would he be? Make a plan for him. Draw a diagram and label parts.

Art Processes:
Painting/crayon/overlay; plan first
Wash outline
Textured background
Trees? Sponge and card strips
Paint large areas first
Class set up alternative applications; limited palette; cleaning without water
Other Learning Activities: Music and Movement: "A Wild Rumpus" (Ministry of Education 1993a, 51); use locomotion words; build up a list for the class.

Dragon world computer programs
Letter to *Dragon of an Ordinary Family* by Margaret Mahy (Mahy 1969)
Riddles collection
Research dragon
Book review
Invention
Treasures – write about something precious to you – *Model*!
Word list
Word search
Shared Book: *The Paper Bag Princess* (Munsch 1989).

Ali is not so sure he can achieve his goal, and the children tell him he has to learn to "persevere" and they will help him. The teacher uses the puppet in a very relaxed, undramatic way and the children are quite matter-of-fact and accepting about this novel switch. They speak to the would-be dragon as if it was a real character. The device has the big plus of enabling some of the shyer children to speak out, to talk about themselves, and to express their ideas and feelings with confidence. The children get to see their teacher trying out what it is like to be someone else, too – again the power of modeling.

This only lasts a few minutes. The teacher sets Ali down to "watch and listen" and now recaps the story the class has been examining closely: *The One that Got Away* by John Parsons (1990). It is a story about a boy called Hiti who has a goal – he wants to catch Hone, a huge eel that lives in the stream. The teacher holds up a large accordionlike book (what New Zealand teachers call a "concertina book") for which the children have all been preparing their own illustrations and text in speech bubbles. This is the class's own version of how the story might have gone and everyone has contributed.

Anne tells the children how pleased she is with their work so far. She opens the book at the title page and exclaims: "Well, look at that! We've even got a copyright sign!" (The children preparing this page had seen the symbol in books and decided they needed one, too!) She reads some of the speech bubbles and comments on some of the illustrations – drawing attention to strong points, praising, coaxing along, always accenting the positive. She then gathers one group of children to work with her and she sends the others off to work on completing their part of the class's concertina book.

The group working with the teacher now begins a more intensive study of the text. This is *guided reading*. She has chosen to work with these particular children today because they are all early readers and she believes they will find this text both challenging and enjoyable. In particular, the teacher wants the children to think more deeply

Teacher Planning

The teachers in this part of the school work together as a team or "syndicate" to assist each other with the planning and organization of their chosen class themes. In order to meet her children's learning needs, Anne has decided that goal setting will be a key focus for this theme study, and she has planned a number of activities based on a story entitled *The One that Got Away* by John Parsons (1990). She has also drawn on some teaching suggestions prepared by Sandra Chandler, lecturer in Social Studies at the nearby Auckland College of Education (Chandler 1992).

The learning outcomes are described as:

♦ To explore a number of *concepts* such as competition, cooperation, self-esteem, perseverance, determination, and satisfaction.

♦ To develop a number of *understandings* or key ideas about human behavior, such as:

   – People gain satisfaction from perseverance in pursuit of goals

   – Some goals are unrealistic and have to be modified

   – It is important for us to have our efforts acknowledged by others

   – Sometimes we need to seek support from others and work cooperatively to achieve goals.

♦ To practice/develop/strengthen a number of *skills.*
   – **Thinking and valuing skills,** such as:
      – Considering alternatives and consequences
      – Group decision making
      – Applying ideas in new situations
      – Generalizing
   – **Study and recording skills,** such as:
      – Chart making
      – Time lines
      – Summary charts
      – Personal recording in goal booklets
      – Listing, grouping, labeling
   – **Social participation skills**, such as:
      – Cooperation in groups
      – Pair and group discussion
      – Following group decisions

♦ **All this is to be demonstrated by:** The children persevering and working cooperatively to gain satisfaction in pursuit of personal and group goals.

Figure 3-4. Children working on the concertina book

about the characters' feelings and to find reasons for their actions. (Reading is about more than "being able to say the words." It is about understanding the text and grasping the meaning encoded there.) While the text meets their individual needs as readers, grouping the children enables the teacher to work efficiently and the children to benefit from the collaborative exploration and discussion. But this is not a "fixed" group. When the learning is complete the group will dissolve, and as the teacher observes new learning needs, new groups

Concertina or Accordion Books

The beauty of the concertina format is that it allows the book to be used in two ways: it can be displayed and read as a wall story when spread out, and when it is taken down, it can be folded up accordion-style and stapled down the spine so it becomes a conventional "big book." In this form it can be stored with all the other class-innovated big books and read by individual children at their leisure or by the teacher from time to time for shared reading. In fact, many of the class's creations become much loved and frequently revisited treasures.

will be formed. This is an individualized reading program which makes use of grouping for shared learning needs.

On a previous day the children had built up a chart with their thoughts on what the boy in the story must have been feeling as he went off to try to catch the giant eel.

"We know what Hiti was feeling. But now I'd like us to do the same for Hone, the eel. What do you think he was feeling at the start of the story?" The children's answers come readily:

"Happy..."

"Relaxed..."

"Satisfied..."

"He's probably a little hungry...!"

Anne responds, "Yes, and then along comes Hiti. What thoughts do you think passed through the eel's mind when he saw this boy standing there looking into the water? Maybe we should go back and check with the story."

She opens the book and a child helps find the place. Anne re-reads the passage for them: "'...and his stomach grumbled and rumbled...'"

Now the children volunteer their thoughts as they try to think and feel like an eel:

"I'm feeling hungry!"

"I'm feeling excited."

Anne replies, "Good. And what thoughts were passing through his mind? What would he say if he could speak his thoughts?"

A child pulling a thoughtful eel-like face says: "I'll get that boy sooner or later!" Everyone laughs and the other children pull eel-like faces.

"Now let's go to the end of the story. How do you think he feels when the line breaks?"

"Pretty upset..."

"Frustrated..."

"Disappointed..."

"Still hungry..."

"What thoughts do you think were going through his head now? What would he say if he could speak his thoughts?"

"I'm going to swim off and tell all the other eels about the hungry boy who got away!"

While this group works with the teacher and begins to fill out the story chart, the other children are also hard at work. The concertina book is spread out on the floor at the back of the classroom, and as each group finishes its illustrations and speech bubbles for their page they paste it in position on the appropriate page.

It is now 10:15 A.M. and the teacher calls all the children to the mat. She quickly reviews the morning's work, praising the children for how their class book is coming along. But now it is time for some music. The teacher leads the children out of the room and across the concrete quadrangle to a room that has been set aside for all the classes in this block as a shared space. It is set up for music, but it is also used for group discussions and as a withdrawal area by the various classes.

Now the class teacher becomes the music teacher. Like all New Zealand elementary school teachers, Anne is a "generalist" – expected to be able to teach all subjects of the curriculum. In fact, music is one of Anne's strengths and so besides providing her own class with a lively music program, she also assists other teachers with help and advice and leads the singing with her guitar when the whole school gathers for the weekly assembly.

Although it is a music period, the class theme is addressed here, too: the children are learning a new song entitled: "You Can Do It." The children are particularly excited about this because their teacher wrote it! A few bars on the guitar and the teacher leads the children into some very robust and entertaining singing.

There is music theory too, as the children clap and sing time names to parts of the song. Next up is a greeting song that makes use of ways of saying hello in numerous languages from around the world. As they sing, one child finds "where we are now" on a world map.

Now it's time for rhythm and the children chant a lively "Dr. Knickerbockers," complete with actions. The children contribute to the class music too: one has brought a recording of her favorite song and she would like the class to sing it. It happens to be "Puff (the Magic Dragon)" (Yarrow and Lipton 1962) and as soon as the children hear it, one has a bright idea: "This is a song about dragons! We should let Ali hear us sing this song!" So one child is quickly dispatched to bring the puppet to take part in the song.

It is now 10:30 A.M. and the class is dismissed for playtime. Anne goes to the staffroom to collect a cup of coffee and then heads outside to supervise the children as the "duty teacher." The whole school is out playing in the playground. Some race to-and-fro on the grass field behind the school. Four children are lying on their backs, head to head, staring up into the blue sky on this clear and warm spring morning. Others cluster round on the concrete areas besides the classroom, contentedly chatting. Adults are liable to call this break from work "morning tea" (although nowadays New Zealanders are just as likely to drink coffee as tea!). For the children, however, this is playtime and many are munching on a snack they have brought from home. There are painted squares and shapes on the concrete, and here and there small groups of children have set up their own games of Hopscotch, What's the Time, Mr. Wolf?, and Four Square.

You Can Do It

Anne walks around holding her cup of coffee and chatting with the children as she goes. Although she is the teacher "on duty," as they say, there doesn't seem to be any need to intervene or do anything with the children apart from observe and enjoy the contact with those who run up to tell her something before darting off to join the other children again.

All the other teachers have gone to the faculty or staffroom. Here they sit and gossip and chat, compare notes on how the morning has gone, and maybe check out meeting times and details of the school program. Apart from the teacher on duty, everyone is here – the teaching staff, the office staff, the principal, two student teachers from the nearby College of Education, and the parent volunteers who have come to the school today to help prepare equipment and assist the teachers. While the office staff are here having morning tea with everyone else, two children sit in the office to greet and direct any visitors and to take any telephone calls.

The break lasts fifteen minutes. A few minutes before it ends, the principal stands and introduces the visitors to the staff. The faculty share a few quick notices about the school sports day, about a combined class field trip, and about a curriculum paper someone thinks others should read.

The school bell sounds and Anne makes her way to the staffroom to leave her cup. Meanwhile the children quietly and independently make their way back into their classrooms. The teachers are making their way back from the faculty room, too. By the time Anne arrives at her room, her class of 35 six- and seven-year-olds have taken out their current writing projects and are already hard at work on their own pieces.

The children receive help with their writing in one-on-one conferences with the teacher. But much of the class instruction in writing comes from regular sessions of write-tos and shared writing, when the teacher will model the writing process and subtly teach the writing skills, strategies, and attitudes she has observed the children are needing. Today is no exception – after a period of time, the teacher calls the children to the mat for some prewriting "brainstorming" and further exploration of the current theme of goal setting. Once again, Ali is called on to help.

"What do you think Ali wants to do? What does he want to achieve? What are his goals?"

The children smile: "Ali wants to be a dragon."

"Oh, that's right! And what does it mean to be a dragon?"

"He wants to act like a dragon."

"He wants to be like a dragon."

Supervision of Children in the Playground

Teachers from the U.S. are sometimes surprised to see so many children being supervised by only one teacher (or two if it is a larger school) during the morning and lunchtime breaks. They worry about accidents and about the possibility of lawsuits against the school for inadequate supervision. New Zealand teachers do worry about child safety but do not have to be concerned about the possibility of a lawsuit if there is an accident: New Zealand has, in effect, a national insurance policy that provides for free medical care in the event of an accident. In return for this, the people of New Zealand gave up the right to sue for personal damages. Of course, there are serious consequences if a child is hurt as a result of, for example, faulty playground equipment or inadequate supervision. But large sums of money do not change hands and so the community interest is more on prevention than on the exploitation of an accident for monetary gain. It also means teachers do not have to be so paranoid about child safety. Sometimes you have to let children take some risks in the interest of acquiring learning experiences. New Zealand teachers would also ask: "How many teachers do you need on duty in order to prevent all accidents?" And of course, there is always the risk of a freak accident. The worst playground accident I ever experienced took place right beside me. It was break time and I was sitting on the seats outside my classroom. Alongside me were some children from my class playing a game of "Statues." In this game you jump off the seat and have to freeze in whatever position you land. One girl jumped off the seat and tripped. She landed on the concrete in front of me and knocked out her front teeth! She was only an arm's length away and yet I still couldn't have prevented the accident.

There are areas of responsibility for children in this matter of safety, too. A U.S. teacher observing in a New Zealand school was startled to see a child who had grazed his knee go to the school sick bay and have it cleaned up and a bandage put on it *by another child!*

"He wants to do dragon things."

The teacher frowns thoughtfully: "But what are the things dragons do? We've all read lots of dragon stories lately. What do they do?"

"Ali wants to be able to fly like a dragon."

"He wants to be able to breathe fire."

"He wants to look fierce and frightening!"

Now Ali speaks up: "Oh! Do I have to be fierce and frightening?"

"Of course! Sometimes dragons eat people! That's why they're frightening."

Another child is not so sure: "Maybe they're only frightening because people think they eat people?"

"I don't think I'd like to eat people," says Ali. "They're all lumpy and bony!" The children laugh.

"What does Ali need to help him be a dragon?" asks Anne as she spreads a large piece of blank paper on her easel.

"He needs wings."

"He needs a fiery breath."

"He needs some sharp teeth."

"Oh?" says the teacher. "And what does he need sharp teeth for?"

"To eat hard stuff like rocks or meat!"

"Or other dragons!"

"Or people!"

Some children have other ideas: "Perhaps he doesn't eat people! He might be a plant-eating dragon! Or live on insects!"

Now Anne is ready to start recording some of these ideas. "I think Ali is going to have to make up his mind what kind of dragon he wants to be. Let's make a list for him of the kinds of dragons he could be. Making a list of ideas is often a good way to get our writing started. I'll write them up but I'll need a helper to ask people for their ideas." Everyone is eager to help and after a thoughtful glance around the class, the teacher chooses Elizabeth. The teacher now begins to write as Elizabeth chooses children with their hands up to volunteer their ideas as to the kind of dragon Ali could be. They come thick and fast: "Ali could be fierce...!" "Ferocious...!" "Helpful...!" "Friendly..." "Cool..." "Mean..." "Ugly."

Anne asks, "What does Ali need to have to help him achieve his goal of becoming a dragon?"

"Spines..." "Scales..." "Toenails..." "Claws..." "Funny horns..." "Flashing eyes..."

Anne: "What about size? How big a dragon do you think Ali should be?"

"He could be fat..." "Skinny..." "Tall..." "Have a long neck..." "Be huge..."

"How would he move as a dragon?"

"Stomp..." "Spring..." "Fly..." "Spiral..." "Hover..." "Lurch..." "Swim..." "Gallop..." "Explode..."

Anne continues: "Where could I find some more movement words if I needed them?"

"In a story..." "A giant story..." "At the learning center..." "In our dictionaries..." "A thesaurus..."

Now she takes another big sheet of paper and writes in the middle: "To achieve my goal I need to..."

The children quickly suggest ideas to fill out the web: "Learn to fly...." "Find out about dragons..." "Decide what sort of dragon I want to be..." "Persevere with flying..." "Keep trying to be a dragon..." "Be a creative thinker..."

Anne looks startled at that one. "A creative thinker? Great idea! Now, how can Ali do all these things?"

"He could get another dragon to help him!"

"He'll need to be systematic."

"He'll need to be persistent..."

As the teacher writes she pauses and "thinks aloud": "Persistent? Is that persist*ent* or persist*ant?* I'd better put an arc over it to remind me to check that out later. Perhaps someone would like to look it up for me?" A child quickly volunteers.

By now both large pieces of paper are covered with ideas. Anne is not only subtly reviewing the social studies theme about goal setting and making connections with the stories they have been reading about dragons, she is also modeling a number of ways of organizing ideas and handling information – such as brainstorming, listing, and using semantic webs. All these are also helpful things to use when writing, so the children are also practicing and learning about aspects of the writing process.

Now the children are sent back to their tables to work on their own writing. Although the children are working on free choice of topic at the moment, it is not surprising that a number are working on imaginative stories about dragons! The children write in their draft writing books. When they are unsure of how to spell a word, they attempt it but put an arc over the word to remind them to check it later.

The children are at different stages in their pieces. Some are brainstorming ideas. Others are doing their first draft. A number are reworking their drafts, proofreading, or revising for meaning. Some are working on the publication version of their piece. This last stage may not only involve concern for layout and presentation but may also include some illustration.

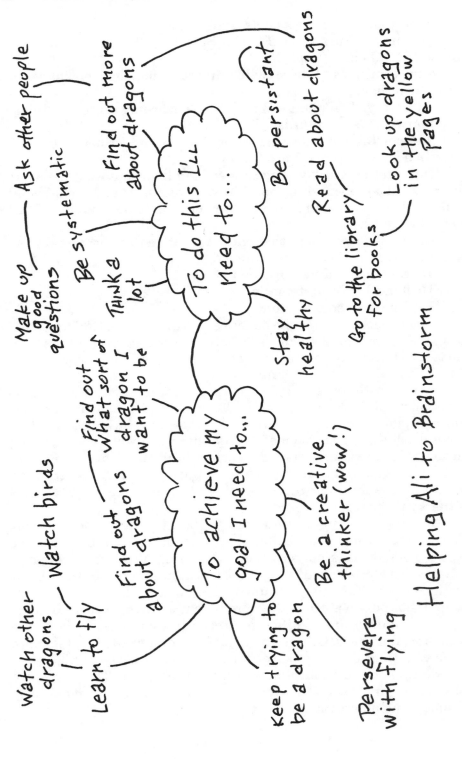

Figure 3-5. Dragon Brainstorm

As they write, Anne now moves among the children, scanning their work, stopping to read and comment, and also to conference and assist where help is needed. The children are used to being "independent writers" and work on their pieces conscientiously and with pride. There's a workshop atmosphere in the room. While they are not "sworn to silence," when children have to speak — maybe to check a piece of information with another child, or to borrow something, or to ask someone else if they would like to read their piece and comment on it — they speak quietly so as not to disturb the others around them. They have learned to respect the needs of their "co-writers."

A Sensible Approach to Spelling

persi͡stent

There are two stages to writing: a composition phase, followed by a publication phase.

The Composition Phase: The writer plans, drafts, and then edits, revises, and refines the drafts of his or her ideas. At this stage it is important to get those ideas down on paper and that means keeping ideas flowing. Having to stop and check the spelling of every word one is doubtful about could well stop the flow altogether. And anyway, at this stage, one is primarily writing for oneself, so as long as the writer can read it, accurate spelling is not so crucial. Instead, teachers teach the children to draw an arc over a doubtful spelling as a reminder to come back and check it later.

The Publication Phase: Once the writer is satisfied with the draft and is ready to share it with the rest of the world, all that changes. Inaccurate spelling (and poor presentation, bad handwriting, and the like) might well confuse or deter the reader. So now the writer checks all doubtful spellings (and learns any words that may be needed again). Care is taken with handwriting and presentation, too — all to ensure the best possible communication with one's readers.

11:45 A.M. The children put their writing away. It is now time for mathematics. The children are working through the Beginning School Mathematics program and as part of a measurement strand, the class is currently focusing on money. First the children gather on the mat with the teacher and begin by reviewing the value of coins and bills (or what in New Zealand are called "notes"). Unlike U.S. paper money, New Zealand bills are different colors, so this is not only about reading numbers on the bills, but being able to recognize the different colors, too.

The teacher now sends the children off to work in a number of groups. The children can read what group they are in on the mathematics board. This magnetic board shows a number of groups – the Triangles, the Rectangles, the Squares, and the Circles. Children's names appear with the groups and alongside are the activities for the day. There is also a section called "Options" and the children know that when they have finished their activities they can choose something from this list, too. Today the Triangles are working on "Fred's Fast Food Machine." The Circles are buying and selling and giving change for household cartons and containers in the classroom shop. The Rectangles have a sheet with a number of problems on it. The children have to work out change for a number of purchases and to show the appropriate coins.

Among the Options list is a pile of junk mail brochures. The children have to cut out a range of objects and then work out how much they have "spent." This activity is also connected to the current goal-setting theme, since the children are also required to prioritize and decide which objects will best help them meet their own personal goals.

Anne doesn't have to elaborate on the mathematics tasks – the children can read them and quickly set to work. First she works for a time with the Rectangles, then moves on to the Circles, and so on. The children discuss what they are doing and if they need help, they first seek it from other members in the group. There is a pleasant, busy atmosphere in the classroom. This is a mathematics time – but it is also a "language" time, too. Language is about ideas – all kinds of ideas, not just literary ideas but also social studies ideas, scientific ideas, physical education ideas, and of course mathematical ideas. The children talk when they need to as they discuss and try out ideas on each other. Voices are just loud enough for those around them to hear but not so loud as to disrupt other children. They stay on task and complete their activities before moving on to the "Options." Often it is hard to find the teacher. For a time she will be on the floor

Personal Goals

As part of this study, the children set themselves some personal goals which they evaluated at the end. This is what some of the children wrote:

At the start of the year, I was not very good at Ballet and I was getting all mixed up. I wanted to leave but Mummy wouldn't let me. But after that I was getting good at it. I achieved my goal by keeping going. Now I am in lots of concerts.

Laura

My goal is to write neatly and hold my pencil properly at the same time. That's easy for some people but I find it hard because I'm left handed. I don't like it when people tease me and say you're not holding your pencil properly. I like it when we did letters to our parents because we promised to hold our pencils properly and I want to keep it up!

Sarah

My first goal was sitting up nicely. I achieved it by trying it. My second goal was running round the field without stopping in fitness. That I am still trying at.

Trista

with the Circles, then she'll be kneeling beside the Rectangles to discuss their work. A little later she'll be on the other side of the room talking to a child, or in the classroom shop making a purchase from the children working on that task.

Lunchtime arrives. The children are responsible for packing

everything away and making sure all sets of mathematics equipment are complete. When they are ready, the children gather on the mat. Even when dismissing the class for lunch, mathematics continue to be interwoven: "All those children wearing blue today may go to lunch... All those children with more than two pockets may go to lunch... All those children who have laces on their shoes may go to lunch... All those children with nice big smiles may go to lunch!"

It's 1:00 P.M. and lunchtime is over. The bell rings and the children make their way into the classroom. They know this is the time for independent reading, or SSR, so they know what to do without having to be told: each child takes out a book, finds a comfortable place, and settles down for a quiet read. Some are sitting at the

Parent Helpers

New Zealand schools have a long tradition of involving parents where possible in the work of the class. This is particularly true of the junior classes, although some schools are fortunate to be able to have help throughout the school, and even high schools make use of parent volunteers. In the past these helpers were usually home-making mothers who were able to spare a morning or afternoon for volunteer work at school. But in recent years more and more "father helpers" have been able to assist in this way. Parent helpers may help prepare classroom materials, cut up paper and cardboard for art, make math and science equipment, cover reading books, and assist the classroom teacher to supervise the children on class excursions and experience walks. In many schools they also read to children, listen to children read, and help with writing and math time. Schools will also organize "working bees" on weekends to help plant shrubs and trees on the grounds and to help with the building and maintenance of adventure playgrounds and outdoor equipment. Parents are also heavily involved in fundraising activities. Most schools have a number of fund-raising activities throughout the year and for many this also includes a "School Fair" or "Gala Day." Parents are encouraged to donate objects for sale and teachers and children help sell them and entertain the crowds.

tables. Some curl up in the classroom library. A number of children stretch out on their tummies on the floor. It is as if there is a "spell" on the class for the next ten minutes – the reading spell.

1:15 P.M. For the rest of the afternoon the class is going to work on an art/craft activity as part of their dragon/goal-setting theme. Anne is now joined by one of the children's parents. She has volunteered to be a "parent helper" with this activity and will stay until three o'clock.

The children have already begun making some magnificent dragons out of clay. At present they are sitting on the classroom windowsill, wrapped in plastic to prevent the clay from drying out. (From time to time during the morning and lunchtime breaks, like visitors to a science museum peering into glass cases, children from other classes have come to stand outside the classroom windows and stare in at these silent creatures.)

The teacher takes one of the children's dragons down and examines it carefully. She comments on the way the clay has been joined, about the strength of the design, and about how the dragon's features have been shaped. "Today we're going to begin to add *texture* to our dragons."

The children have encountered the word *texture* a number of times lately and the teacher writes it up on a list of high interest

Figure 3-6. A Child's Dragon

"Theme Words." Although this is a craft activity, there is constant discussion, negotiation, and as ideas are developed, vocabulary grows.

"What can we use to make scales for our dragons?" The teacher has assembled a range of "tools" – nails, screws, pieces of patterned plastic, and so on. She demonstrates how to push them into the clay and build up a pattern. The children suggest other texture tools they could use. They are clearly enthralled by the whole project and keen to start, so now the classroom becomes the art room. New Zealand primary schools do not have specialist art rooms. Art is integrated with everything else the class does and takes place in the classroom. (Of course, they don't have specialist art teachers either – the teacher is the art teacher.)

First, to protect their clothing, the children have to put on their "art smocks." These are ingeniously simple: each child has brought from home an old shirt belonging to his or her father or older brother. With the sleeves cut off and the buttons done up it makes an excellent artist's smock!

Now the work begins. The children unwrap their dragons and set about experimenting with texture ideas. The teacher has donned an old shirt, too, and with the parent helper, moves around the classroom, talking with the children, observing what they are doing and helping them when they need it. The children share their ideas with each other. This is art and craft – but it is also science (speculation, observation, hypothesizing, experimenting, confirmation or modification of hunches, and so on), social studies (learning to work together cooperatively), and of course it is language – but language with purpose and a wide curriculum context. Later the children will write about their discoveries and read about them.

At 2:40 P.M. it is time to "pack up." Anne calls the class together and quickly moves about the room praising and commenting on the children's creations. The comments are specific and critical. This has been a learning session and she is reviewing, highlighting, and applauding their discoveries. The children are given five minutes to put everything away and clean up. The dragons go back into their plastic bags, art shirts get put in a box, hands get washed, and newspaper that is re-useable is folded up and put away. As they finish restoring their areas to "normal," the children move to sit on the mat. The teacher doesn't need to direct this activity – it is the children's responsibility and they handle it efficiently and with a minimum of fuss. While she is waiting, the teacher picks up her guitar and quietly strums. She begins to sing softly – almost to herself. The children sing along quietly too. Soon everyone is gathered on the mat and they all join in with their theme song:

> *"You can do it! You can do it! You can!*
> *You can do it! You can do it! Do or die!*
> *You can do it! Just plan and work through it!*
> *You can do it if you try!"*

Their voices trail away. The teacher puts down her guitar and looks around the room and smiles. It's been a good day and the children are obviously pleased, too. She asks the children to think of something they have done today that has made them feel good – something special they may want to remember.

"I liked working on my dragon..."

"Making the scales..."

"Our book..."

"Talking to Ali..."

The teacher picks up the puppet alligator and sets it on her hand. "Thank you for all your help, girls and boys," says Ali. "I've learned so much about being a dragon today. I think I'm a little closer to achieving my goal."

The bells rings. Anne says, "Good afternoon" to the class and dismisses them. They start to move toward the cloakroom to collect their

---

Teacher Commitments

Today is the one school day Anne doesn't have an after-school meeting or an inservice course! It is a revealing indication of the teacher commitment Anne, like most New Zealand teachers, takes for granted. After school her week is like this:

Monday:	Syndicate meeting (1 hour)
Tuesday:	Staff meeting (1 to 2 hours)
Wednesday:	Senior Management Team meeting (1 hour)
Thursday:	Inservice course (2 to 3 hours)
Friday:	Her one free day!

bags. There is no rush to leave. They chat in twos and threes. A couple of children hold back to talk to the teacher. Some of the children have class duties: the two window monitors set about closing the windows; another child cleans the blackboard. Children from other classes move past the classroom windows and pause as they go to point to the dragons on the window ledge. The teacher thanks her parent helper and heads off to the faculty room to collect a cup of herb tea.

Anne returns to her classroom nursing her cup. At last the room is quiet. She gathers up the children's writing for the day – no, her day is not yet over... She has a notebook beside her in case she wants to record any comments on the children's writing. She takes a mouthful of hot tea, then picks up the first story and begins to read...

Chapter 4

Organizing for Learning: Inside a Standard 3 and 4 Classroom

Welcome to Leigh Primary School

Figure 4-1. Leigh Primary School

Leigh Primary School is a country school situated on the coast, about an hour and a half drive to the north and east of the city of Auckland. The setting is idyllic. The school perches on the top of a grassy rise with commanding views out across the ocean to Goat Island, where there is a marine research station, and beyond to the blue outline of Little Barrier Island. In summer this is a popular place for holidaymakers, but now, in late autumn, most of the seaside cottages that cluster here and there on the road down to the beach are empty. Behind and on either side of the school are rolling grass-covered hillsides where farmers keep dairy cows and run sheep. The University of Auckland maintains the Leigh Marine Research Laboratory on Goat Island and this is now the largest single employer among the parent community. Other employment includes farming, saw milling, and fishing. The district boasts a few shops, a church, a fire station, a service station, a hotel, and two community halls.

The school roll is small. There are three teachers for the 78 children who come each day.

School 4: Leigh Primary School

Location: Small school in country district
School Type: A "contributing primary school" – one that takes children from Junior 1 (age five) to Standard 4 (about age ten)
Roll: 78 students
Staff: three
School Organization: The school is organized into three classes: a New Entrants/Junior 1 and 2 composite; a Junior 3 and Standard 2 composite; and a Standard 3 and 4 composite.
Community Involvement: Parents take a lively interest in the school and assist in the classrooms with clubs and school events like sports days.

Leigh Primary School has three classrooms. Each has its own teacher, but the school as a whole has the atmosphere of a big happy family. All three classes are "composites," i.e., made up of more than one class level. Martin Turner has all the senior children in his composite – some 28 Standard 3 and 4 children. Besides teaching this class, he is also the school principal and so there are times when he has to be out of the classroom to see to school matters. He expects the children to be able to work on their own without always having to have the teacher tell them what to do. That is one of the first things visitors notice when entering the room – just how responsible and independent these children are. In addition, as the school's senior students, the children have a number of schoolwide duties.

The Class

Class Level: Standard 3 and 4 composite (two class grades together)
Teacher: Martin Turner
School: Leigh Primary School

Equivalent U.S. Grades: Grades 4 and 5
Years Students Have Spent at School: 4 to 5 years
Ages: 9 to 11 years
Number of Children in the Class: 28
Student Composition:

Ethnicity	*First Language*
25 New Zealand European	English
2 part Maori	English
1 from Cook Islands	English

Martin Turner's classroom has the feeling of a comfortable and rather homey (in New Zealand we'd say "homely") living room. The children have their own individual desks but these are clustered informally, some on their own and some in twos, threes, or fours. There is carpet on the floor and often the children seem happiest working down there rather than at their desks. On the floor they can spread their books and resources about them. The children are used to being free to sit or move around the room and there is a relaxed informality in the classroom atmosphere, but at the same time they are very polite and respectful toward the teacher and toward each other.

Along one side of the classroom is a wall of windows with a panoramic view across the school playground and out to sea. Ample evidence of children's learning is on display around the room. On the

Figure 4-2. Martin Turner's Classroom Displays

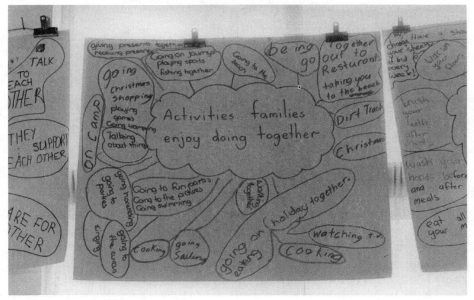

Figure 4-3. Concept Maps

front wall are dye and wash posters depicting greetings from around the world in bright cheerful colors – *Kia ora, Bonjour, Fakalofa Atu, Guten Morgen, Dosvadania*. Other material on display includes mental or concept maps from a family theme study, a class mural from a mangrove swamp study, and posters listing the days of the week, the months of the year, and the number names in Maori.

To one side of the room is a storage area for books, workshop materials, and paints, papers, and other art and stationery supplies. This also includes a sink bench and vinyl-tiled preparation area for the more "messy" art and craft activities. The back wall of the classroom has two large sliding doors which can be pushed back to allow this room and the classroom next door to be used as one large combined space. There is also a library corner and a computer center with two PCs. A roster sheet with all the children's names on it makes sure all the children get a chance to work here throughout the day.

It is 8:20 A.M. The children who come on the first bus are already at school. A few who live within walking distance are here as well. Some children are in the classroom organizing their books and papers. Some are out in the playground bouncing a ball and playing pass and catch games. A local farm dog wanders across the concrete netball court. The teachers are in their rooms, setting out their resources for the day. A parent holding a baby drops off her five-year-old. She has a quick word with the teacher and then leaves.

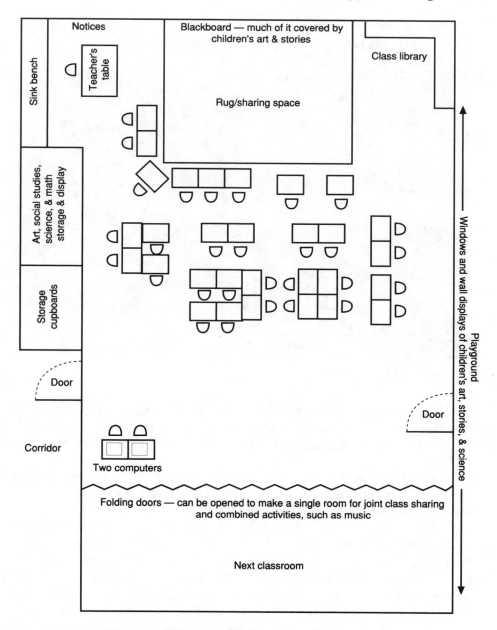

Figure 4-4. Diagram of Martin Turner's Classroom

Figure 4-5. The school bus arrives

The children wander freely in and out of the classroom. One child saunters up to the teacher, who is organizing some books for reading. The teacher stops to chat for a minute, then carries on. The child stays to help.

At about 8:30 A.M., all the teachers leave their rooms and gather in the staffroom. This is a morning ritual – a chance to grab a quick cup of coffee and exchange any notices.

It is now 8:40 A.M. and the school bus returns with its second load of children. They clamber off, clutching their schoolbags. Most are also carrying their bathing suits wrapped in a towel. (To New Zealand children these are not "bathing suits" but their "swimming togs.") The school has its own swimming pool and throughout the warmer months of the year swimming instruction is part of the New Zealand school curriculum. The teacher of language, mathematics, science, art, music, social studies, physical education, technology, and health also becomes the swimming instructor and coach!

The school bell rings and all the children gather in a sheltered corner of the playground for the regular morning assembly. They sit together on the warm concrete while, up front, the principal sits on the seat outside one of the classrooms. Behind him are two large murals that were planned and painted by the children. He greets the school in Maori and English. The children respond. He introduces the school's visitors for the day and then shares some important notices. He praises the children for the care they are taking with the school environment. Some children have their names mentioned for the interesting work they are doing in their classes. Everything says this is a family gathering and throughout the atmosphere is relaxed, positive, and supportive. Even a couple of morning "growls" are presented positively as a health issue and a "challenge" for the children.

Five minutes have passed and now it is time for fitness. This happens every morning, so the children know what to do. Everyone takes part in this, and they all do it together – the five-year-olds alongside the ten-year-olds and everyone else inbetween. They spread out in small mixed teams across the school playground. They do some preparatory stretching and then it's, "On your marks, get set, go!" and they're off into a vigorous but fun relay with everyone running to-and-fro. No sooner has everyone had a turn than the whole school is off in a wild fun run around the playground and straight into school.

Figure 4-6. Assembly

The children in Martin Turner's classroom all know the morning routine. First up it's time for reading. Today the entire class is doing sustained silent reading. Everyone is prepared for this. They take out their books and settle down for a good private read. The teacher roves, taking the time to quietly talk to the children about their books as he goes.

Typical Daily Schedule

8:50 – 10:00	School Assembly
	Fitness
	Reading
10:00 – 10:40	Mathematics
10:40 – 11:00	Break
11:00 – 12:30	Language (Spelling, Handwriting, Poetry, Creative/Formal Writing)
12:30 – 1:30	Lunch and Break
1:30 – 3:00	Theme (Social Studies/Science/ Music/Art)

Variations: Periods of Physical Education, including swimming; Taha Maori (Maori culture studies)

When the reading stops it's time for mathematics, although today Martin has a test he wants the children to do.

It is now 10:40 A.M. and it is time for the morning break. Outside it is a warm autumn morning, and the children get their playlunch from their bags and wander outside to eat their morning snack and play for fifteen minutes. The teachers, meanwhile, gather in the staffroom for a quick cup of coffee. One teacher goes out to be with the children and to supervise the play.

It is now eleven o'clock and the bell rings again. The children eagerly make their way back into the classroom. Martin gathers the children on the rug in the front of the room. According to the timetable, this would normally be a language block, but the children are working on a number of projects in different subject areas and there aren't enough resources for all the children to do any one of these activities altogether at the same time. So he has decided to make the rest of the day a "U PLANET" day (i.e., "You plan it"). What this means is that the teacher puts up a list of all the things he wants the children to accomplish today, but the children can decide in what order they would like to do these things. This means the children can take responsibility for their own learning and plan how they are going to use their time to make sure they complete all that is required of them. To make this even more demanding, a number of the activities have to be done with partners or in small groups, and this means the children will have to negotiate with each other in order to schedule their time and plan their day. As they complete each activity they are to write the appropriate symbol on a large class list. It helps the teacher keep an eye on what everyone is doing, and because it is a kind of public record, it also helps keep the children motivated and focused on the day.

A major task for today is the completion of the current theme activity. This is an art project. The children have been working together

---

Testing and Assessment in the New Zealand Classroom

Testing plays a very small part in the New Zealand classroom, but at the start of the year teachers may have their classes complete Progress and Achievement Tests (known to New Zealand teachers as PAT tests) for diagnostic purposes. The teacher wants to get a quick overview of the class and some idea of the children's strengths and weaknesses in mathematics to use as a basis for his or her planning. But what is more important, the teacher is also observing the children closely and keeping samples of the children's work so he or she can document their progress and share this with the parents. The test results will ultimately play a very minor part in the overall assessment and evaluation of the child's learning. Observations of the child doing the "real thing" are regarded as far more important than data derived from the contrived or simulated behavior available in a test situation. The teacher uses checklists as prompts for the observations and will note things the child is able to do consistently, things the child is starting to be able to do, and things that the teacher has not seen the child do yet or seems ready to do. The results of any testing the teacher or school may do is regarded as something for professional interpretation and use by the teacher. The results would certainly not be made public or, as in parts of the United States, be published in the newspaper. New Zealand teachers would be horrified at the thought of such crude assessment instruments being accorded so much deference and credibility.

in pairs to present a mixed-media representation. Before setting the children off to begin planning and executing their self-choice day activities, Martin leads the children in a review of the work they have done so far on this project.

"Well, artists, let's have a look at what we've done so far." From the pile of children's artwork on the floor beside him the teacher picks up a large sheet of paper and places it on the easel beside him so all can see it. U.S. teachers would probably think this was a very large picture – the paper is about three feet high and about four feet across, yet the ideas cover the whole page with ease. The theme for the activity is "faces in the crowd." The design for the whole picture has been carefully worked out, but this is "work in progress" – while some faces are obviously complete, or nearly complete, a large number are still at the draft sketch stage.

"This is Dylan's and Chris's, isn't it?" The two children nod. For this art activity all the children are working with partners. Instead of being the product of an individual imagination, each picture is a shared creation, an act of collaboration. Dylan and Chris had to plan it together and discuss and evaluate their ideas. At times they had to negotiate, to find ways to reach decisions when they disagreed, to make compromises, to listen to each other, and to support each other. To make this possible, the picture has first been drafted in outline in chalk. It's a very useful medium for this kind of collaborative exercise because it can easily be dusted away as ideas are rejected or modified. It also enables the children to work quickly and to think about the overall design and balance of the picture. The teacher looks at the picture thoughtfully and the children examine it carefully, too.

"They're not all looking out in the same way, are they? Some of the faces are in profile. I think that makes it more interesting, do you agree?" The class murmurs its approval.

"And look what they've done with perspective, too. Some of the faces are in the foreground and some seem to be standing further back. That's good thinking, too." The teacher points to one face where there is a grey pallor showing through the pink face tones. "The skin color here is interesting. Would you like to tell us how you did that?"

Dylan explains: "We put the grey on first, where the cheek is. Then we put the flesh pastel over the top and sort of rubbed it in. You have to be careful not to smudge it too much or to get the smudging on anything else."

The next picture has an interesting assortment of crowd characters. The teacher points to a Modigliani-like face. "Now look at the shape of this head. That's a very interesting use of distortion, Kate and Sophie. Sometimes exaggerating features like that can make us see them as they really are. Remember those paintings we looked at the other day?"

The discussion continues. The children join in with positive and perceptive comments about each other's work. In this classroom "studio" they are all artists, all with different talents but all equal in their right to express their ideas.

"There are different kinds of people."

"Different ages, too."

"There's some old people and then there's a baby."

"There's even an *alien!*"

The children laugh, but then they look closer and discover that it's true — one of the people in this particular crowd is a science fiction "alien" and no one had noticed.

The teacher works through each picture, sometimes leading the discussion, sometimes letting the children lead. The children are exploring the properties and possibilities of mixed media — using pastels with crayons, crayons with colored pencils — so this is clearly an art lesson. Yet the teacher is not an art specialist as such. Also, like all good New Zealand teachers, he seeks to make learning a holistic experience, so the children will be able to make connections between what they learn in one subject area and what they learn in another. Besides this being an art activity, it also helps develop the children's language and thinking skills. Health and social studies also play a part in this people theme, and as this is a country school, the idea of a "crowd" has heightened novelty and interest for these children.

The teacher has yet another reason for doing this activity. It is the start of a new teaching year, and he wants the children to generate some artwork that they can display on the classroom walls. He wants them to feel this is their space (in Maori, their *turangawae-wae*), and to feel they have contributed to the learning environment.

"Not everyone will be able to work on the paintings at the same time. We don't have enough space in the room. So partners are going to have to plan their day together to make sure they are free at the same time and that they have enough time to finish everything they have to do."

And so the class begins the planning for the rest of the day. These are empowered learners who know what their tasks are and know it is up to them to prioritize and organize their time. As for the teacher, he is "on call" all day. When he is not assisting children with inquiries, he works with particular children in need. As in most New Zealand schools, children with special learning needs are "mainstreamed" or "included" in the regular classroom. This class is no exception and to-day the teacher is able to give a lot of one-on-one help to the two special needs children in this class.

After lunch there is one interruption to this student-planned day: the class adjourns to the school swimming pool for a swimming lesson. Now the generalist class teacher becomes the swimming coach! Most New Zealanders live within 50 miles of the sea and even inland there are rivers and lakes, and water sports generally are very popular. As a result, water safety and being able to swim are considered very important. Most schools have their own small swimming pool, and during the warmer months of the year – from about late November through to late March – schools will organize regular swimming sessions for each class as part of the physical education program.

After the swimming lesson, the children change back into their clothes and return to the classroom. The contract symbols are beginning to grow alongside the children's names on the wall chart. As the assigned tasks are completed, the children then move onto optional activities. Some help other students with their tasks. This is a self-helping, self-supporting community. By the end of the day everyone has completed their tasks and most have moved into optional tasks as well.

As the bell rings for the end of the day, the first school bus arrives for its load of children. The teacher dismisses the children who go on the first bus. The others remain behind to help display the now-completed "Faces in a Crowd." Even though the school day is over the children continue to discuss their learning. They examine each other's paintings and talk about them as they find spaces on the wall to display them effectively. Martin is outside supervising the children boarding the bus. A parent arrives to collect her family and stops to chat with him. By the time the second bus has arrived, the children have all the artwork up. The teacher returns to the now silent classroom and examines their handiwork. The other two teachers wander in to have a look, too. They always compare notes on what is happening in each other's rooms.

Martin Turner is pleased. "Yes, they have done a pretty good job today. Maybe tomorrow I'll get Jayd to make a caption for the artwork..."

Chapter 5

Making Links: Inside a Form 1 and 2 Classroom

Welcome to Howick Intermediate School

Figure 5-1. Howick Intermediate School

Howick Intermediate School is an older and reasonably affluent middle class suburb of metropolitan Auckland. Thirty years ago it was separated from the rest of the city by a belt of farmland, but all that was eventually swallowed up in successive waves of land subdivision and house building. Previously this tended to be a rather monocultural suburb, with most families of Caucasian background. (New Zealanders would probably use the Maori word *pakeha*.) But in the last ten years an interesting development has been an ever-growing number of families who have emigrated from Hong Kong, Korea, Taiwan, and other parts of Asia. Unlike most previous immigrant groups, these have tended to be more affluent and thus able to make choices about where they wish to live. They come to settle in Howick for many reasons, but one of the main ones is the high reputation of the local schools like Howick Intermediate. As a result, the schools are becoming more culturally diverse and interesting. The proportion of Asian students at Howick Intermediate is currently about 12 percent and is continuing to grow.

School 5: Howick Intermediate School

Location: City suburb
School Type: Intermediate (See page 124)
Roll: 640 students
Staff: 31, including a principal, deputy principal, and associate principal
School Organization: All the classes in the school are "composite" Form 1 and 2s. New students join a class in Form 1. This means that in each class half the students will be Form 1s and thus new to the school, and half will be in their second year with the teacher (Form 2s) and thus "old hands." The policy of mixing the classes in this way means that the experienced students can help the new students settle in, and they in their turn will help the next year's intake of new students. It also helps build a sense of community. All classes are organized heterogeneously, i.e., there is no attempt to track or stream or group according to ability.
Staff Organization: The staff is organized in six teams with three to four classes in each. A senior teacher is responsible for each team. All classes belong to class clusters or a family group called a *whanau.* Whanau is a Maori word that may be loosely translated as "family," but it also includes one's extended family and friends and "support group." The teachers in each whanau work together on planning, preparation, and organization, and their classes may join up for subjects like physical education, music, and technicraft (a composite "subject" that embraces practical work for boys and girls in woodwork, metalwork, cooking, and fabric crafts). There will also be opportunities for formal and informal sharing in such activities as sports, language, and music. The whanau system provides support and community for both teachers and students.
Community Involvement: The school enjoys strong community support. Parents contribute to and participate in many aspects of the school program. Volunteers provide language support for children needing extra help, assist with the school lunch program, and help with class trips and school sports days.

One of the special features of the school is its fine music program. Besides classroom music, many children play musical instruments in

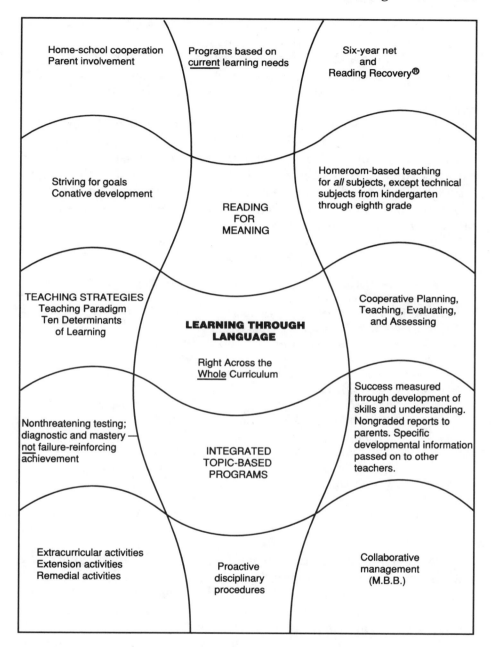

Figure 5-2. Howick Intermediate's Philosophy and Practice. Courtesy of Principal Brian Pittams.

the school orchestra or sing in a number of the school choirs. These rehearse during the lunch hours or after school. On Saturday mornings the school is a center for a community instrumental music program and children of all ages come from all over the local district to learn from instrumental tutors and make music in a range of groups and ensembles.

The school also benefits from a very competent and stable staff with strong professional leadership from the principal and senior teachers. Philosophy and practice are seen as connected and interwoven. Principal Brian Pittams has summed up this interlocking relationship with the diagram on page 103. The key facets of the school's structure, philosophy, and teaching practice reinforce each other to make up a kind of "tapestry."

The Class

Class Level: Form 1 and 2 composite (two class grades together)
Teacher: Bev McNaughton
School: Howick Intermediate School
Equivalent U.S. Grades: Grades 6 and 7
Years Students Have Spent at School: 5 to 7 years
Ages: 10 to 13 years
Number of Children in the Class: 36
Student Composition:

Ethnicity	*First Language*
26 New Zealand European	English
3 from Hong Kong	Chinese
2 part Maori	English
1 part Samoan	Samoan and English
1 from U.S.	English
1 from South Africa	English
1 from Korea	Korean
1 from India	English

Bev McNaughton's classroom has the feel of a comfortable, busy, and rather crowded workshop. In size it is definitely small, and with 36 adolescent bodies and desks, there isn't much space to spare. Each student has his or her own individual desk but these are clustered together to make a number of group tables. The desk tops are detachable and when the children are working in groups, they often pick up their desk tops and carry them to some part of the room where there is space. The children like to work on the floor, too, especially for group work, and so they are able to use their mobile desk tops as convenient writing surfaces.

At the "front" of the room is a carpeted space for class sharing.

Figure 5-3. Bev McNaughton's classroom

At the back of the room there is a sink bench and tiled area for "wet" activities (although artwork such as clay modeling and painting will take place anywhere in the classroom – the children are used to spreading newspaper before commencing "messy" work). The teacher's desk is over to one side, up in the front of the room, and there is also a library and quiet reading space in the opposite corner.

The walls are covered with a great variety of students' work. Some is mounted on tables and even more hangs from the ceiling. This includes:

- students' poetry and creative writing
- students' concept mapping on earth science
- students' book reviews, articles, and projects
- students' artwork (paintings, posters, diagrams, information webs – and in a wide range of media such as paint, crayons, collage, charcoal, pencil, mixed media, and so on)
- lists of interesting words and vocabulary fun
- book displays
- science displays
- the menu for the day (setting out the teacher's plan for the day's schedule)
- memos, reminders, and notices about class and school activities

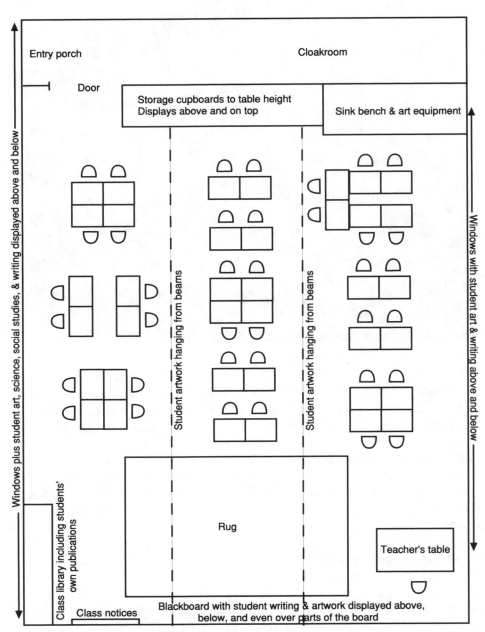

Figure 5-4. Diagram of Bev McNaughton's Classroom

A Typical Day

It's eight o'clock in the morning and Bev McNaughton's students are beginning to arrive at school. Most walk from their homes in the local neighborhood. Some are dropped off by parents on their way to work and some come on bicycles. The teacher is already at work, putting up some notes on the blackboard and sorting out materials for today's sessions. The children hang their coats and bags in the small cloakroom in the lobby to the classroom. The weather forecast is for showers today and most of the children have brought raincoats. It never snows in this part of the country so raincoats are the main item of "extra" clothing that needs to be hung up. The cyclists all have their cycle helmets (compulsory in New Zealand), and the children also carry a schoolbag for their homework, the books they're reading, and of course, their lunch.

The children come into the classroom as they arrive. They greet and chat with Bev and with each other in a relaxed and informal way.

At 8:30 A.M. a bell sounds, although it is really an unnecessary reminder – all the children are here ready to start. They collect to-

---

School Uniforms

In this school all the children wear a school uniform. This is a decision the parents have made, and it probably reflects a community belief that school uniforms help raise the school "tone" or "discipline." Very few New Zealand primary schools have school uniforms, but most intermediate schools do and nearly all secondary schools have school uniforms of one kind or another. It is a custom that probably harks back to certain English school traditions, but it also reflects the prevailing concern among New Zealanders about being egalitarian and nonelitist. To American teachers it often seems quaintly contradictory for a community with an education system that places so much emphasis on individualized child-centered learning to want all the children to look the same! However, it would be wrong to assume that everyone in New Zealand is happy with school uniforms, for it is a subject that continues to be debated with considerable heat.

gether on the carpeted sharing space at the front of the room. The teacher sits on a chair and what is a predictable morning ritual begins. First the roll is called. The teacher greets each child using a variety of languages:

"Aloha, Nicole."
"Aloha, Mrs. McNaughton."
"Kia ora, Jason."
"Kia ora, Mrs. McNaughton."
"Good morning, Monna."
"Kia ora, Mrs. McNaughton."

The children respond, sometimes in the same language, but always in their language of choice – some like Monna in Maori, some in Nuean or another Pacific language, some in Korean, and of course, some in English. The teacher marks them "present" in the class attendance register.

Typical Daily Schedule

8:40 – 10:55	Language (oral discussion, reading, writing)
10:55 – 11:15	Break
11:15 – 12:30	Mathematics
12:30 – 1:30	Lunch and Break
1:30 – 1:45	Sustained Silent Reading
1:45 – 3:00	Theme (Social Studies/Health Education/Science/Art/Music)

Variations:
Periods of: Physical Education
Music Assembly
School Assembly
Technicraft (art or metalwork, woodwork, or cooking)
Library

The morning "class meeting" continues with a quick overview. Bev has drawn up a plan for the day on the blackboard, and at this point she quickly runs over the events and tasks and their time frames. As she goes, she recaps on work in progress:

"I know most of us have a number of things to finish off. Aaron and Gareth, you will need some extra time to complete your topic pieces. May and Jason may need some conference time with me today, too..." She uses the words "we" and "our" a lot, and there is a clear assumption in all this that the work of the day is everyone's responsibility, not just the teacher's.

First up, it's shared reading. The teacher sits on a student's chair

Figure 5-5. Shared reading

holding a large format book so all can see the beautiful illustrations. The children, all 36 of them, sit huddled about her on the mat. Some sit up straight, cross-legged. Others wrap their arms round their knees and hug them as they listen to the story. Two girls lean against each other. One boy, deep in thought, rests his chin on his hand – his elbow wedged against his knee. Some, still concentrating hard, sprawl. Getting your body comfortable can sometimes be difficult when you're somewhere between the ages of ten and thirteen and some of you are clearly starting to feel the signs and strains of that adolescent growth spurt. A visiting U.S. teacher might find this an extraordinary scene: shared reading on the mat using a big book with children of this age? And for that matter, a class of 36 students made up of two different grade levels with an age range of ten to thirteen years?

And what's more, they're loving it. There is a sense of pleasant ritual here. All the children are engrossed. All eyes are on the book. All ears are tuned to the teacher's quiet and intimate voice. It is almost as if they are primordial cave dwellers, huddled round a fire. Only the warmth comes from the story:

"Long ago when the world was new, there lived a young man named Enora. Enora and his people lived in a rain forest filled with wonderful food. Delicious fruit hung on the trees and the rivers were full of fish'" (Meeks 1991).

The teacher reads on. Her quiet yet warm voice draws the children in. You can almost see them straining forward as they listen. As the story unfolds, the drama begins to build. Every now and then she stops to ask a question. It's a natural pausing and seems to fit in with the rhythm of the story. These are not "test" questions. There are no right or wrong answers. Instead they nudge along the children's reflection. She challenges them to predict, to enter into the feelings of the characters, to hypothesize, speculate, consider.

"Has anyone got any ideas about where in Australia this story might be taking place?"

"It can't be inland, outback."

"How do you know?"

"The tropical forest. It would be dry and dusty."

"There wouldn't be any trees."

"Maybe near the coast because of the fish."

The teacher continues to read, "'Once again the colors appeared and moved among the birds. Before long they came toward Enora and touched a tall thin bird standing close to where he was hidden. Enora threw his stick and hit the bird on the neck. As the bird lay on the ground, the color ran from its feathers. The other birds disappeared, leaving Enora alone in the clearing.'"

The teacher silently examines the illustration. The children are quietly thinking about it, too. She turns the page. "'He rushed forward, seized the dead bird and ran into the rain forest. When Enora reached the camp he ran straight to his mother, calling to her that he had proof of what he had seen.'"

There is a hurt sigh from the children as they appreciate the enormity of what the character has done.

"What do you think his mother and the others are feeling?"

"They're angry."

"Hurt."

"Alarmed."

"What is it that makes you think that?"

"The way they hold their hands in the illustration."

"Their eyes."

"'Enora knew he would have to return to the clearing. When he arrived, the birds silently made a space for him. For the last time the colors appeared and flowed over the birds. Before long Enora was surrounded by birds with feathers of every color. But Enora's feathers remained black.'"

The story has ended. The teacher quietly closes the book. One child in the front reaches up to stop the closing for a second, eager to check something out. No one moves. They're still caught up in the atmosphere of the story. It is as if the story is going on silently inside their minds.

Bev judges the mood, lets it ride a little, then draws them back to the class theme and the task for the morning. She suggests some other legends the children might like to read for themselves. Some of the children have suggestions, too. One mentions a film he has seen. Another comments on a sequence seen on a TV documentary. For these children it is clear that learning is about making connections.

Now the teacher introduces a group activity to follow the story. "We need groups of about five people. You'll need a facilitator, a recorder, a collector, and a reporter."

She shows them some photographs which she has mounted on light poster board. These are not commercially produced photographs but materials the teacher has collected herself. New Zealand teachers have always been very resourceful when it comes to making or adapting classroom learning materials. This "do-it-yourself" tradition partly has come about because schools have not had a great deal of money to spend on materials and equipment, but also because teacher-made materials are more likely to be more appropriate because they are tailor-made to meet the specific needs of that particular class.

"I want you to look closely at what the people are doing in the photographs, and I want your recorders to note that down. But I also want you to think about why they may be doing, what they're thinking; and I want you to note that, too. I want this to be a quick brainstorm so I'm only letting you have ten minutes for this. So recorders only need to write notes — just enough so the reporters will be able to give the class a fair idea of your group's discussion and conclusions. Ten minutes means we'll all meet back on the mat again at 9:20."

The children stand and move off without any fuss or noise. Bev doesn't need to organize the groups – the children are used to forming quick groupings like this and they rapidly assemble into clusters of about five. Roles are speedily agreed upon, and each group chooses a space in the room and sets about the task in hand. Some sit at desk clusters. Others sit on the floor – some bringing their desk tops with them so they will have something to write on. One group settles into the library corner. The children talk quietly and there is a buzz of voices (sometimes New Zealand teachers call these "buzz groups"). They listen to each other, and the group facilitators make sure everyone has a chance to express their ideas. Meanwhile, the teacher roves, observes, conferences, moves on...

"Where is this taking place?" asks one facilitator. The others crowd round and examine the photo closely.

"It can't be in the rain forest because the trees look brown and dry."

"I think it must be somewhere near the coast."

"Could be, but why?"

"The size of the trees. They're big. There must be enough rainfall to grow that big."

"I think he's right. Look at the foliage."

The time is up. The teacher claps her hands quietly – just twice. The children fall silent and turn politely to listen. "Thank you. Let's hear how you got on. I'd like you to bring your sheets of paper and your photographs with you." The children make their way back to the mat.

This is part of the constant tidal flow that functions in this classroom throughout the day. The teacher brings the class together for a sharing of ideas and for class instruction. The children are then sent off to study stations around the room where they work independently or in groups. The teacher moves among them, listening, taking part when she feels the need to prompt the children's thoughts or to refocus the children's understanding of the task. Then the class is called back together again for more sharing and instruction.

The groups now present their ideas to the whole class. The first reporter presents his group's conclusions: "We're not sure, but we think this is a singing group for some ceremonial purpose."

"Oh, yes?" says Bev. "That's interesting. And why did you think that?"

"Well, they have a didgeridoo. That's a ceremonial instrument. It's not like – well, you know how we'd have someone with a guitar just playing for entertainment. Also their faces are painted."

Students from other groups contribute too: "The man carrying the pouch – that might contain hunting tools or some medicine."

"It's obviously something old. Not something modern. It's made of animal skins or maybe the bladder of an animal. It looks to be something traditional."

The teacher directs the discussion back to the group: "So that's your hypothesis, it's a ceremony...?" (The teacher uses the word "hypothesis" frequently. To hypothesize is an important skill for science, social studies, mathematics, and for thinking and problem-solving generally.)

Figure 5-6. The group reports to the class

The recorder for the group now sums up their conclusions: "We think it shows a kind of ceremonial dance and it probably tells a story they want to remember, a legend."

The discussion goes on. Each group presents for a few minutes and then the other children respond, sometimes agreeing, sometimes disagreeing, but adding points, interpretations, hypotheses. Bev's contributions are rich with positives: "Good point," "That's very relevant," – and she reflects their ideas back to them for reconsideration: "So you think the houses they made were not very strong?"

The children respond thoughtfully: "They probably didn't have to be."

"Why was that?"

"They moved around a lot."

"They only used them for shelter and sleeping."

"And it didn't rain much either."

There's humor, too. One child observes: "They look kind of like stick igloos."

But the teacher keeps them thinking. "Right. And what do igloos and the aborigines' stick houses have in common?"

"They're easy to make."

"They use the materials that are all around them."

Now the teacher puts up a statement for the children to consider:

"The aboriginal people are very resourceful." She tells the children she wants them to go back to their desks and think about that statement and then she wants them to write down their ideas and responses. They leave the mat and once they reach their seats, they sit and begin to think about the statement. There is silence in the room. Some begin to write. Others stare into space before they pick up their pens. Everyone is "on task." Across the front of the room are the large information webs that each of the groups has prepared. This is a chance for each to review their own learning. It's also a useful recap for this block of work time.

Break time arrives. Bev dismisses the class. The children make their way outside, but there is no rush. Some chat and gossip in twos or threes in the room. Two children remain at their desks to work on a theme project they are keen to have finished. The teacher leaves the room and crosses the concrete quadrangle between the classrooms. Now there are children gathering. There is laughter, greetings, a game begins.

The bell rings at 11:15 A.M. and the children make their way back into the classroom. It's time for mathematics. Today is a practice and extension day and the students will work from the only textbook the class has. (In fact, the mathematics text is the only textbook used in New Zealand primary schools. Even then, rather than use it slavishly, New Zealand teachers generally will use it only as a guide and as a useful source of examples.) The teacher does some practice examples on the blackboard and then sets the students to work. Most of her teaching in this block today will be one-on-one teaching with children needing special help. But she is not the only source of help. The children whose first language isn't English know they can always get help from their class buddies (although sometimes in mathematics the help goes the other way!).

At 12:20 P.M. the teacher reviews the math learning and books are put away. There are a few minutes until lunchtime and she takes this opportunity to share some poems with the children. She reads a couple of her favorites and then asks for requests. The children have lots of favorites and sometimes they join in with the reading.

12:30 P.M. is lunchtime in this school and after they have eaten lunch, many of the children make their way down onto the grass playing field to play a number of games. Someone gets a softball game going. Out in the middle of the field a game of cricket begins. Other children join in. Some children lie on the grass and gossip. Despite the weather forecasts for rain, it is in fact turning into a warm day and all the children are wearing their school regulation sun hat.

Sun Hats

New Zealand has a very high incidence of skin cancer and so schools are keen to ensure children know how to take precautions against the harmful effects of the sun. They even have a song about it that tells them to "slip, slop, slap, and be happy!" To translate, you slip into something like a T-shirt, you slop on some sunblock, and you slap on a hat!

A teacher on duty walks by from time to time. The children run up and talk to him. Another teacher comes down and joins in the children's game of softball. It is very relaxed.

1:30 P.M. and the bell sounds. The children make their way back to their classrooms and take out their own personal reading books for ten minutes of independent reading. The teacher has her book, too, and all one can hear in the class is the combined breathing of 37 people engrossed in the enjoyment of reading. After a few minutes of modeling, the teacher leaves her book and begins a quiet conference with one of the children.

The rest of the afternoon is given over to a social studies theme study on Maori life before the Europeans arrived. The emphasis is on the wise use of resources and so the theme will reach beyond social studies into cartography (linking with an earlier study of map making), science (care for the environment), literature, and contemporary current events (in particular, a recent settlement of a dispute over Maori fishing rights).

The teacher begins with an activity that brings together a range of knowledge and skills from previous studies: "Today I want you to start by imaging what it would be like if you belonged to a Maori tribe and you were pushed out of your area by another tribe – let's say it is a more aggressive tribe so you decide to look for a new place to settle, a new place to build a *pa* (Maori fortified village). What kind of things would you be looking for?"

The answers come quickly and thoughtfully: "Fresh water."

"Good food supplies."

"A place where there are lots of trees."

Bev picks up on this one: "That's interesting, Jason. Why trees?"

"To build houses and palisades. And canoes, too."

"Excellent."

"They'd also need high ground for a lookout. And preferably near the sea, seeing that is where danger is liable to come."

"What kind of danger?"

"The canoes of any warrior neighbors!"

And so the discussion goes on. Sometimes Bev asks a question. When a student suggests the need for a rugged coastline, she asks: "Perhaps you could elaborate on that for me." But most of the time the teacher *receives*: "Good," "I like that idea," "That's an interesting idea," or "You're all really on the ball today."

The teacher now shows them a photocopied contour map. All the map depicts is the land, the sea, and the topography. The children are quickly divided into groups and given the task of planning a pa site on this landscape. To do this they have to hypothesize what there might be there, and then use their theories to justify why they have chosen to use the site in that way. The children talk, ponder, discuss, try out ideas on each other, agree, disagree, make suggestions, ask each other to clarify, praise, and applaud. What the teacher models so effectively the students now continue with each other.

Ten minutes later a vast range of ideas have surfaced and interestingly, every group has come up with a completely different location! Each group quickly presents their choices to the class and gives a précis of their justifications.

Now the teacher pushes the activity further: "Earlier we talked about the things you would need for a good pa site. Now I want you to go back to your project folder and I want you to draw your own map showing the ideal site for a pa. If you want trees for construction of shelter, then mark them in on your map. If you would like sandbars for gathering shellfish, then mark that in, too. Think about the balance of resources, too, and about the generations who will come after you."

This is a tall order and the children are delighted. They quickly set to work to construct their maps, finding ideal sites for the location of the *whare* (houses), the *kumara* (sweet potato) gardens, the fishing grounds, the lookouts, the protective fortifications, and so forth. The teacher circulates and assists and after a few minutes, stops the class again.

"Adam has just reminded me that last year's Form 1 did an exercise in mapping and we made a list of the kinds of things that help make for a good map. Adam thought it might be helpful if we went over these. Thank you, Adam. That's an excellent idea. For the benefit of this year's Form 1, who can remember some of the things we talked about last year?"

Class Counselors

Each class in the school elects its own class representatives to attend regular meetings with the principal and senior staff to discuss schoolwide issues and contribute to school planning and policy decisions.

"A good map has a frame."

"A scale so you know how big or small or far away everything is."

"Bearings so you can work out where the sun comes from."

"A grid in case you want to give reference points."

With this information, the children resume their work. This is an individual exercise but that doesn't stop cooperative work happening: the Form 2 children are obviously more experienced with this kind of activity and several take it upon themselves to go and help the Form 1 students. This is not 36 students working on personal projects – this is an interdependent collaborative learning community!

The class begins to pack up at 2:50 P.M. Some of the children have finished their maps and have already begun to fasten them into their project folders. Others put their maps in their bags to take home to complete in their own time. This class has set homework, too. The tasks are on the blackboard and the teacher quickly reviews them: some spelling words to review, some mathematics to finish. The teacher has some other reminders, too: "We need someone to clean out the mouse cage, class counselors need to prepare for their meeting, the room needs to be left tidy, and bring some *raupo* if you can" (a kind of flaxlike grass needed for a Maori weaving and kite-building activity).

Bev thanks them for the good day. They leave, clutching their bags and the things they need to do their homework. They chatter and gossip. A few stay behind to talk with the teacher for a few minutes. The last one leaves and the room suddenly seems very empty...

Part II

New Zealand
Classrooms in Context

Chapter 6

How Are New Zealand Schools Organized and Managed?

Questions from American Educators

In Part I we looked closely at five specific classrooms in five different New Zealand schools. But American teachers and administrators will want to know about the wider picture, too, such as what options are available to New Zealand parents with school-age children and how the New Zealand school system is organized and managed. They'll want to know what teachers are expected to teach and something of the historical background to all of this, too. In this section I try to answer some of these contextual questions.

How do New Zealand children get their schooling?

New Zealand has a national public education system which is funded by central government from taxation and other revenue.

♦ Most New Zealand children attend the free public schools.
♦ Some will attend private or "independent" schools (which still receive some assistance from the State but the parents are expected to pay fees).
♦ Some will attend "integrated" schools (which are "private" schools that have elected to become integrated with the state system; they are state funded and thus free but may have a religious or special character).
♦ Some may be educated at home. Parents may choose to "home school" their child and currently some 4,000 New Zealand children are home schooled. Sometimes this is a parent choice but sometimes it is due to health reasons, because the family lives in a remote area, or because the child has been expelled from school as a

121

result of serious misconduct. Children may also be enrolled in the "Correspondence School," which provides lessons via the mail and radio.

At what ages do students start and finish school in New Zealand?

Most New Zealand children start school at the age of five (although it is not compulsory until the age of six). School is compulsory up to the age of sixteen, but most students will stay on until about their eighteenth year.

What are the early childhood education or "preschool" options?

Early childhood education is entirely optional and there is a wide range of choices for parents. Depending on what is available in the district, these choices may include: kindergarten (public and/or private), playcenter, Kohanga Reo, Pacific Island language nests, and child care.

Kindergarten: The use of the term "kindergarten" in the New Zealand setting may be confusing for U.S. readers. In New Zealand a kindergarten is a "preschool" institution – usually for children between the ages of three and one-half and five years (although the term "preschool" is sometimes frowned on because it implies that whatever happens in the early childhood years is merely a preparation for the "more important" school).

There are state-funded public kindergartens that are free and private kindergartens where parents pay fees to enroll their children. Parents can enroll their child in a public kindergarten from the age of three years, although when they actually start will depend on the

---

The New Zealand Education System: An Overview

Early Childhood Education–birth to age 5
Primary (including Intermediate School)–age 5 to about 12
Secondary School–approximate ages 13 to 18
Tertiary Education–University, polytechnics and Institutes of Technology, Colleges of Education, and other providers

places available. For some public kindergartens, for example, parents have to put their child's name down on a waiting list until a space becomes available. Children attend for half-day sessions, five days a week. It is usual for children to start kindergarten by attending the afternoon sessions first and then move to the morning sessions as they get older. Private kindergartens generally are run on very similar lines. Enrollment age for private kindergartens varies but in the main they are very similar to those provided by the State.

Playcenters: These are early childhood education settings which are run in effect by the parents on cooperative lines. Parents enrolling their children are also required to assist with the supervision and running of the center. The playcenter movement also trains parents to be playcenter supervisors who manage and run the daily sessions with rostered parent help. They, in turn, help and train new parents to be supervisors.

Kohanga Reo: Kohanga Reo is an early childhood education setting where the Maori language is the main language of instruction and where Maori culture is central to the program. The term means literally "language nests" and Kohanga Reo have been very successful in keeping the Maori language alive. They have also been very powerful in strengthening children's self-esteem and learning pride. In the process, their learning in all areas of the curriculum has benefited, including their English! While the program in Kohanga Reo emphasizes Maori culture, the children attending are by no means exclusively Maori.

Pacific Island Language Nests: These are early childhood education centers where the language and culture of a particular Pacific Island community is paramount.

Child Care: In addition to the above there are a range of crèches, daycare, and other child care centers that take care of children for parents while they work or study.

What are the elementary or primary school options?

In New Zealand, elementary schools are called "primary" schools, which may be *full* primaries and thus cater to children ages five to twelve, or *contributing* primary schools that cater to children from age five to about age ten. The children from contributing schools go on to spend the next two years at an intermediate school, although these are considered to be part of the primary system too.

Primary school children start as "New Entrants," then pass through Juniors 1, 2, and usually 3 (sometimes still called Stan-

A Full Primary School – Juniors to Form 2		
Starting Age	*Equivalent U.S. Grade*	*New Zealand Class Name*
5	Kindergarten	New Entrant/Junior 1
6	1	Junior 2
7	2	Junior 3/Standard 1
8	3	Standard 2
9	4	Standard 3
10	5	Standard 4
11	6	Form 1
12	7	Form 2

dard 1). They then metamorphose into Standard 2 children and make their way through the standard classes, year by year. They complete their primary schooling with a year in Form 1 and a year in Form 2.

When a school only goes up to Standard 4 (a contributing school), the children will then go on to an intermediate school for two years. Intermediates are something of an historical anachronism. They were begun in the 1930s at a time when the majority of New Zealanders left school after Standard 4 and went to seek a job. Intermediates were begun as an attempt to try to entice the populace into higher education. The hope was that they would become like the American junior high schools and students might attend them for, say, four years before going on to a high school, but secondary schools were reluctant to give up their control of the third and fourth form years, and so the intermediate schools never managed to grow beyond two years of schooling.

A Contributing Primary School – Juniors to Standard 4		
Starting Age	*Equivalent U.S. Grade*	*New Zealand Class Name*
5	Kindergarten	New Entrant/Junior 1
6	1	Junior 2
7	2	Junior 3/Standard 1
8	3	Standard 2
9	4	Standard 3
10	5	Standard 4
		↓ ↓ ↓
		Intermediate School
11	6	Form 1
12	7	Form 2

A Historical Note about Terminology

The term "junior" or junior class is relatively new. Forty years ago, the children would have entered what was termed the "primers" and gone from Primer 1 through to Primer 4. The origins of this term go back to the start of New Zealand schools, when the junior class was determined by the book level or "primer" the child was able to read. With New Zealand's high reputation in reading being based on a rejection of basal reading schemes like this, it's probably just as well that we no longer use this terminology.

While American children move up the "grades," New Zealand children move up the "standards" from Standard 1 or 2 to Standard 4. The term "standard" also began in the early days of New Zealand education, when children had to take an examination at the end of each year to determine whether they were up to the right "standard" to graduate to the next year's class. The exam was set and administered by school inspectors who galloped about on horseback from school to school.

After Standard 4, children move into Form 1 and then Form 2, and this "form" terminology continues to be used through the secondary school years. For its historical origins, you have to go back to the schools of nineteenth-century England, where children were often made to sit on benches or "forms." When they showed they had learned all their lessons, they were "promoted" to a higher "form."

What are the secondary school options?

At about age thirteen, students go on to a secondary school. Terminology can be a little confusing for U.S. teachers – most secondary schools call themselves high schools, such as Pukekohe High School or Onehunga High School, but quite a number of secondary schools call themselves "colleges." Edgwater College, Rangitoto College, and Rongotai College are all secondary schools catering to students from Forms 3 to 7 and should not be confused with tertiary or university "colleges" as they exist in the United States. (And just to make it even more complicated, some of our tertiary institutions call themselves colleges too, such as Auckland College of Education and Lincoln Agricultural College.)

A Typical New Zealand Secondary School		
Starting Age	*Equivalent U.S. Grade*	*New Zealand Class Name*
13	8	Form 3
14	9	Form 4
15	10	Form 5
16	11	Form 6
17	12	Form 7

Although secondary education usually caters to Forms 3 to 7, currently there are moves for some secondary schools to provide some tertiary courses as part of an "eighth form" concept, and in some districts there are Form 1 to 7 schools.

There are also "area schools," usually found in more remote country districts, which cater to the whole school age span, from New Entrants through to Form 7.

What are the tertiary options?

Approximately one in three New Zealand students goes on to pursue some form of tertiary study beyond his or her high-school years. For many this will mean attending a university and pursuing a traditional degree. But large numbers will also attend a variety of courses and programs offered by polytechnics, technical institutes, and other providers. Those wishing to train for teaching will attend a College of Education (see Chapter 8).

What is the academic year in New Zealand?

The academic year in New Zealand corresponds roughly to the calendar year, with schools opening for the year in February and concluding the year in early December. Traditionally schools have used a three-term year, but after much public debate, as of 1996 all New

A New Zealand Form 1 to 7 Secondary School		
Starting Age	*Equivalent U.S. Grade*	*New Zealand Class Name*
11	6	Form 1
12	7	Form 2
13	8	Form 3
14	9	Form 4
15	10	Form 5
16	11	Form 6
17	12	Form 7

The New Zealand School Year (as of 1996)		
January February March	Summer break continues Term 1 begins	Semester 1 begins
April	Term 1 ends Two-week break Term 2 begins	
May June July	Term 2 ends Two-week break Term 3 begins	Semester 1 ends Study break Semester 2 begins
August September	Term 3 ends Two- or three-week break Term 4 begins	
October November December	Term 4 ends Summer break begins	Semester 2 ends

Zealand schools will have switched to a four-term, two-semester yearly pattern.

What is the length of a typical day in a New Zealand school?

Primary schools usually start at nine o'clock in the morning and conclude at three o'clock, with a morning break of about fifteen minutes and a lunch break of an hour. Secondary schools may start at 8:30 A.M. – many with a morning school assembly, and usually conclude at 3:30 P.M.

How are New Zealand schools governed and managed?

Central government, through the Ministry of Education, has the overall responsibility for the provision of education in New Zealand, but each school is governed and managed by its own individual Board of Trustees. All Boards of Trustees must include the principal, staff representatives elected by the teachers, and in the case of secondary schools, student representatives elected by the students. The remaining board members, and by far the majority, are parents. They are elected by the parents of the students attending the school (and not by local taxpayers, as might happen in some parts of the United States). As a result, those most directly concerned with the students' education and welfare have the most say over how the school is run.

The Board of Trustees is charged with the responsibility of "governing" the school. This means the board consults with the principal and teachers to determine broad policy and to appoint staff. In addition, it is responsible for the finances and efficient running of the school. On the other hand, the principal, assisted by the teachers, is entrusted with the task of "managing" the school and providing an effective learning program for all students. This division between governance and management is difficult to define precisely but in practice works well. In most communities throughout New Zealand there is effective cooperation and collaboration between schools and boards, teachers and parents.

Furthermore, as funding comes not from local taxes but from the central government and is based on a formula determined by the number of students, the wealth (or poverty) of the local community has no *direct* impact on the school's budget. The result is a high degree of fairness and equity in the way education is provided throughout the country.

However, it is also necessary to concede that the socioeconomic status of the local community may have an *indirect* impact, in that schools in more affluent areas may be able to call on a wider base of community expertise to assist with the running of the school than those in less affluent areas. They may also be more successful in their own local fund-raising drives. (This extra fund raising would be for additional educational facilities or amenities over and above that provided by central government. It might include large items such as a school swimming pool, or it might be for more books for the school library, extra computers, or sports equipment.) While site-based management of schools is generally considered to work well in New Zealand, this is an aspect of the system that has caused some concern.

Other responsibilities of the board include consulting with the principal and teachers in order to establish the school's goals and policies and taking responsibility for the school property, personnel, and finances (with the exception of teachers' salaries, which usually come directly from the Ministry.[1]) The trustees also have to help the school

---

[1] Currently there is considerable debate on the issue of who should pay the teachers and how. The government would like to bulk fund the teachers' salaries and encourage schools to pay teachers according to performance. Teachers and large sections of the community are suspicious of this, fearing that the resulting competition between teachers will make them reluctant to collaborate and share ideas and resources.

communicate with the community, and when necessary, they have the task of appointing a new principal.

The principal's role is to "manage" the school, to provide professional and educational leadership, and to see that the school's policies are put into action. The principal also makes recommendations on staff appointments.

How are New Zealand schools evaluated?

All schools and early childhood education centers are evaluated at regular intervals – usually about every two years – by the Education Review Office. These inspection visits result in two different types of reports: an "assurance audit" and an "effectiveness review."

The *assurance audit* is an assessment as to how well the school is complying with all legislation and regulations and gives background information on the school (e.g., size, ethnic mix) and information on how well the school is managing such things as the curriculum, student support, Maori education, staffing, and finance. It may also give suggestions for improvement.

The *effectiveness review* provides an overview of student achievement and measures this against the goals the school has set for itself. These reports are available to the public, and parents are encouraged to read them.

How do parents choose a school for their child?

Parents have the right to send their child to any school in New Zealand provided the school is not overcrowded. When the school roll grows too large, the school must create an enrollment scheme with declared criteria for student selection. Usually this is geographic, but other criteria may also apply (for instance, if a child has a brother or sister who is already enrolled in the school).

What about children with special learning needs?

The right to enroll a child at any school applies to all children, including children with disabilities or special learning needs. Children with special learning needs are included in mainstream education in New Zealand, and when possible they are taught along with all the other children by the classroom teacher. The philosophy of child-centered learning means that the program is adapted and modified to meet the needs of the individual child, rather than the child having to fit in with or adapt to the classroom program.

This also means that children are not retained for a further year at any particular class level, nor are they ever accelerated to a higher grade level. As discussed in Part I, the first three years of a child's schooling are handled in a very flexible way, and the children may change classes at any time during the school year. Once children have moved into Standard 2 (at about eight years of age), they remain with their age cohort for the rest of their primary schooling.

Furthermore, while New Zealand teachers recognize that children have different learning styles, rates, and needs, they are reluctant to give them labels such as "learning disabled" or "gifted." Regarding the former, teachers would argue that one should start from what the child can do, assessing and evaluating their *abilities*, rather than their *disabilities*. Regarding the latter, New Zealand teachers would be inclined to argue that all children are in fact "gifted" and need recognition for what makes them unique.

Chapter 7

What Do Schools Teach?

The New Zealand Curriculum Framework

New Zealand has a national curriculum for all subjects. These are statements that define the learning principles and achievement aims and objectives which all New Zealand schools are required to follow. But the national curriculum does not spell out everything students need to know. Instead, it provides a "framework" and teachers and schools are expected to work with their local community to flesh it out and create their own school curriculum. This will embody the national curriculum but will also take into account local needs, priorities, and resources, the strengths of the teachers, and the special learning needs and strengths of the children.

The New Zealand Curriculum Framework defines learning in terms of seven "Essential Learning Areas" (Ministry of Education 1993b). These describe in broad terms the *knowledge and understanding* which all students need to acquire.

The Essential Learning Areas: Knowledge and Understanding

> Language and Languages
> Mathematics
> Science
> Technology
> Social Sciences
> The Arts
> Health and Physical Well-being

The *Curriculum Framework* also sets out the "Essential Skills" to be developed by all students, and these span across all the learning areas.

The Essential Skills

> Communication Skills
> Numeracy Skills
> Information Skills
> Problem-solving Skills
> Self-management and Competitive Skills
> Social and Co-operative Skills
> Physical Skills
> Work and Study Skills

Finally, the *Curriculum Framework* indicates the place of "Attitudes and Values" in the school curriculum.

Attitudes and Values

Attitudes are defined as "feelings or dispositions towards things, ideas, or people which incline a person to certain types of action" (Ministry of Education 1993b, 21). Attitudes toward learning are considered very significant because they empower the learning, but teachers' expectations, parent and community support, and the students' motivation all play an important role in this, too.

Values are defined as "internalised beliefs or principles of behaviour held by individuals or groups...[and] are expressed in the ways... people think and act" (Ministry of Education 1993b, 21). The curriculum statement acknowledges that no school is value-free and that much is learned from the students' experience of the total environment rather than through direct instruction. However, it is expected that school practices and procedures "will reinforce the commonly held values of individual and collective responsibility which underpin New Zealand's democratic society" (Ministry of Education 1993b, 21).

It is interesting to see how, over the years, changes in emphasis with regard to these three areas (knowledge and understanding, skills, and attitudes/values) have impacted our notions of what learning is. Some fifty years ago, knowledge ruled supreme and learning (and education) was largely defined in terms of what you knew and understood. In the last twenty years or so we have heard a great deal of talk about the importance of "skills" or what you are able to do with your knowledge. Perhaps now we are hearing more about how empowering or de-powering attitudes and values can be in the dynamics of learning. We are becoming increasingly aware that what you learn and how well you learn is often very largely determined by (a) how you feel about the learning and about yourself as a learner (i.e., your attitudes), and (b) by what you expect or believe (i.e., your values).

Chapter 8

```
◨◪◪◪◪◪◪◪◪◪◪◪◪◪◪◪◪◪◪◪◪◪◪◪◪◪◪◪◪◪◪◪◪◪◪◪◪◪◪◪◨
```

How Are New Zealand Teachers Trained?

```
◨◪◪◪◪◪◪◪◪◪◪◪◪◪◪◪◪◪◪◪◪◪◪◪◪◪◪◪◪◪◪◪◪◪◪◪◪◪◪◪◨
```

Colleges of Education

Historically, teacher education in New Zealand has come to be concentrated in a number of specialist teacher education institutions. Over the years they have undergone a number of name changes – from Training Colleges to Teachers Colleges and currently they are mostly known as Colleges of Education. (The exception is the former Hamilton College of Education, which is now a School of Education in the University of Waikato.)

These Colleges of Education prepare teachers for all areas of teaching:

- Early childhood education (educators working with children from birth to five years of age);
- Primary teacher education (teachers working in primary and intermediate schools with children from age five to about age twelve);
- Secondary teacher education (teachers working with students from about age thirteen to eighteen or nineteen);
- Postcertification programs for teachers in specialist areas such as special education and Reading Recovery®;
- Inservice curriculum and school management programs to meet the needs of teachers in their regions.

Early childhood educators and primary school teachers usually complete a three- to four-year program of study and may graduate with a Diploma of Teaching and a bachelor's degree. In general, to train for secondary teaching, students must first complete a three- to four-year degree at a university and then complete a one-year postgraduate program at a college of education.

133

Figure 8-1. Ali Goodall in her very own classroom

How are New Zealand's primary school teachers trained?

Meet Ali Goodall. Ali is a recently trained teacher, and while there is no such thing as a "typical" teacher, her course of study is representative of what most teachers now have to do to become "certified." (New Zealand teachers would say "certificated" – the word "certified" to New Zealand ears implies officially insane!)

After watching her own children growing up and assisting them through the New Zealand school system, Ali decided she, too, would like to be a teacher. Her first challenge was to secure a place at her chosen College of Education. Ali completed the detailed application form, submitted her curriculum vitae, and provided the required references. She was then invited to an interview, where her suitability for teaching was further evaluated. The selection process for those who wish to study to become teachers is rigorous and demanding. The Ministry of Education allocates funding to the colleges based on school population predictions, so there is a limit to the number of places available and this can make gaining admission to a teacher training program highly competitive. For example, at the Auckland College of Education where Ali wanted to study, over half the applicants for primary teaching are turned away each year.

But Ali was successful, and in due course she received a letter offering her a studentship at the Auckland College of Education. In February of the following year she began her six-year journey to her very own classroom and to registration as a fully trained teacher.

The broad outline of her study program was as follows:

Ali's First Year of Study for Primary Teaching

- ♦ Basic courses in language,[1] mathematics, science, and art
- ♦ More advanced courses in language, mathematics, and music
- ♦ Studies in education (philosophy, sociology, child psychology, and pedagogy)
- ♦ Professional practice throughout the year with two blocks (one each semester) of four to six weeks in a school observing and teaching alongside a mentor teacher

---

Ali's Second Year of Study

- ♦ Basic courses in health education and social studies
- ♦ More advanced courses in language, science, and music
- ♦ Studies in education (philosophy, sociology, child psychology, and pedagogy)
- ♦ Professional practice throughout the year with two blocks (one each semester) of four to six weeks in a school observing and teaching alongside a mentor teacher

---

---

[1] "Language" covers instruction in oral language (speaking and listening), written language (reading and writing), and visual language.

Ali's Third Year of Study

♦ More advanced specialist courses in music and music education
♦ Optional advanced courses in all curriculum areas, including language

Ali's Fourth Year of Study

♦ More advanced courses in Maori, science, and mathematics
♦ Computer education and music
♦ Studies in Education (philosophy, sociology, child psychology, and pedagogy)
♦ Optional advanced courses in all curriculum areas, including language
♦ Professional practice throughout the year with two blocks (one each semester) of four to six weeks in a school observing and teaching alongside a mentor teacher
♦ Graduated with a Diploma of Teaching and a Bachelor of Education
♦ Began applying for teaching positions toward the end of the year and was accepted for a position at an Auckland suburban primary school

Ali's Fifth Year

♦ Ali began her first year of teaching. Throughout this year she is supported and assisted by a teacher in the school who is appointed as her tutor teacher. She is also given release time each week for the purpose of consultation, observation, planning, and professional development.

Ali's Sixth Year

♦ Ali continues her teaching, but without an allocation of release time as in the previous year. Like all other teachers she has her class all day every day of the week.
♦ At the end of the year Ali is finally able to register as a fully certificated teacher!

Like all students enrolled at the Auckland College of Education, Ali was able to make choices about subjects she wanted to specialize in. As a result every student has a unique personal study program. Nevertheless, there are a number of "themes" running through Ali's course program that are very typical of the preparation for teaching in primary and intermediate schools in this country.

Some Common Features in New Zealand Teacher Training

♦ **Everyone is trained as a "generalist," able to teach every subject**
Thus, Ali was required to do basic courses in every subject of the New Zealand primary school curriculum.

♦ **Teachers are also able to develop areas of personal specialization**
Ali chose to develop her interest and expertise in music, science, and language to a more advanced level.

♦ **Language (see page 11) is considered to be a very important area of study**
This is demonstrated by the number of compulsory courses in basic language and the opportunity to do extension and advanced studies in this area.

♦ **Specialist studies in education (philosophy, sociology, child psychology, and pedagogy) are a continued theme throughout teacher education**
For at least three of the four training years Ali pursued compulsory studies in education, but these studies were also "applied" in all the subject courses. It is no coincidence that the word "education" appears repeatedly in course descriptions, such as "health education," "language education," "music education," and so on.

♦ **Importance of practical classroom experience is stressed throughout the training**
For three of the four years, Ali spent four to six weeks every six months in a classroom observing and teaching alongside the classroom teacher. Here she was critiqued and supported by the class teacher and also by college lecturers, who would visit her at least three times during each of the teaching practice periods in order to discuss and help her improve her teaching.

These are called "teaching experience" or "teaching practice section" blocks and students are directed to choose a variety of different settings over the course of their study. The college requires students to include at least one each of the following: a junior class (New Entrant, Junior 1, 2, or 3), a middle school class (Standard

2, 3, or 4), a senior school class (Form 1 or 2), a single-cell class-room, a variable-space classroom, a multicultural school, an in-termediate school, and a normal school experience. The schools where Ali did her school experience blocks illustrate this diversity of settings:

Ali's School Experience			
School	*Time Spent in School*	*Class (Grade) Level*	*Type of Experience*
Takapuna Normal Intermediate	3 weeks	Form 2	Normal school; intermediate
Bayfield Primary	4 weeks	New Entrants	Variable space; junior class
Paremorema Primary	4 weeks	Standard 3	Multicultural experience; middle school
Mangawhau Primary	4 weeks	Standard 3	Single cell classroom; middle school
Epsom Normal Primary	6 weeks	Junior 2	Normal school; junior class
Albany Primary	6 weeks	Standards 2 and 3	Variable space, composite (multi-age) classroom; middle school

In addition to the teaching experience blocks each six months, Ali had many other school contacts as part of her regular college classes. All college courses have a blend of theoretical and practical aspects of learning, and most include visits to schools and the observation of senior teachers at work. Many college courses also require students to do "micro-teaching," when the students work with groups of children under the supervision of their peers and college tutors.

Finally, the value placed on practical experience and effective-ness is also evident in the selection of the teaching staff at Colleges of Education. Advertisements for teaching positions at a College of Education will often ask for "evidence of recent successful teaching experience" as an important criteria for appointment.

The end result of all this emphasis on practical experience as a vital part of teacher training is that student teachers not only know the theory but can make it work in the classroom.

Other Questions U.S. Teachers Often Ask about New Zealand Teacher Education

How do teachers get a teaching job?

Every individual school in New Zealand is governed by its own Board of Trustees made up of the principal, elected parents, and teacher representatives. It is their responsibility to advertise when the school has a vacancy and to select and appoint the successful applicant. Vacancies are advertised in local newspapers as well as nationally in *The Education Gazette.*

How are teachers regarded by the community in New Zealand?

Surveys of public opinion show that teachers are held in high regard in New Zealand. A recent survey showed that teachers were among the most respected and trusted of professionals. Concerns about education tend to be global rather than specific. One survey showed that when people were asked if they were concerned about education in this country they said, "yes they were." But when they were asked what they thought about their child's teacher or school they tended to be very happy.

Who pays the teachers?

Teachers in public or state schools are paid by the central government from money that comes from national taxes. A significant proportion of the salaries paid to teachers in private schools is also paid by the State.

What are teachers paid?

In U.S. dollars, a first-year teacher in New Zealand with a bachelor's degree and after four years of training would earn about $18,000 per year. A senior principal in a large primary or intermediate school could earn up to $40,000 per year. For comparison purposes, on average, a New Zealand plumber earns $18,000 per year, electricians earn $19,000 per year, and an average police constable (officer) would receive $29,500.

How do teachers become principals or senior administrators?

To gain a position as a school principal, teachers must first and foremost be effective classroom teachers. The usual path for promotion is to seek a "senior teacher" position, then secure, say, an assistant principal or deputy principal's position, and finally gain the position of principal. The main criteria for promotion is one's effectiveness and professional leadership, not the passing of a few examinations in administration theory. Appointments to these positions are made, like all teaching appointments, by the school's Board of Trustees.

How are teachers graded or evaluated in New Zealand?

Individual teachers are no longer graded or evaluated in isolation. Instead, the Education Review Office conducts regular audits of schools (see page 129). Teachers are evaluated as part of the overall evaluation of the schools, and if a teacher is not effective it is regarded first and foremost as the school's problem to solve for itself.

Chapter 9

How Did the New Zealand Reading and Writing Classroom Come About?
Some Historical Background

The Early Years, 1877 to the 1940s

Free compulsory education began in New Zealand in 1877 with the passing of the Education Act. Prior to that date, if children attended school, they were most likely to be taught to read using the *Bible* or other religious material, but once education became compulsory and schools began to be established all over the country, Church and State were kept separate. Children were taught to read using "readers" imported from England and Scotland, such as Collins's *Readers* and Nelson's *Royal Readers*. These approached reading in a simplistic and orderly fashion – usually they began with the letters of the alphabet and then progressed to two-letter words, then three-letter words of one syllable, and so on. It was another twenty years before locally produced reading material began to be used in New Zealand schools, but this, too, was modeled on the English readers.

The way reading was taught didn't change very much either in these early years. The great-grandparents of today's children were drilled in their letters and letter sounds, and were also encouraged to memorize common words that were "unphonetic." The latter was termed the "look and say" method, but "phonics" was the predominate approach. The whole class would frequently read together, chanting a passage in unison. The children were encouraged to be "expressive" – although instead of expressing the meaning, this really meant copying the exaggerated intonation patterns set by the teacher. (An important school subject was "choral speaking" and reading frequently served this end.) Good posture and deportment were often taught along with reading (see Figure 9-1).

141

THE CARE OF THE BONES.

Just as the twig is bent, the tree's inclined.
                                    —Pope.

There is an old story about a man who took his little son out walking with him one morning in the apple-orchard. Presently they came to a very crooked tree.

The man called to his gardener to bring a team of horses and a strong chain. Soon the gardener came with the horses and the chain.

The father ordered the gardener to put the chain around the crooked tree and fasten the horses to it, to see if the tree could not be straightened.

The gardener did as he was told, and the horses pulled with all their might, but they could not make the slightest change in the trunk of the tree.

How not to carry a Child.

Presently the gardener said, "It's no use, sir, trying to straighten the tree now. It's too late. It should have been taken when it was young and tied up to a straight pole, and not allowed to grow crooked. When it is grown you cannot change its shape."

This was just what the father wished his son to hear, to teach him the importance of beginning to grow properly in his youth.

This is a very good story to remember when we are learning about the skeleton. It is plain to see that the form of the body will be just what the shape of the skeleton is, for upon that all the fleshy part of the body is laid.

If we wish to be erect and to walk properly we must take great care of the bones.

The bones are very soft and easily bent during childhood. It is during this time that the habits are formed which make the body straight and beautiful, or crooked and unsightly.

How not to sit.

As a baby's bones are very soft—just like gristle, in fact—he should not be allowed to lie in an unnatural position. If he is learning to walk he should not stand too long, for the weight of his body will bend the soft bones of his legs, which will become "bandy," as we say, and can never be straightened.

The child who slides down into his seat, the one who bends over his book, or the one who stoops over when he walks will not have a straight backbone.

What do you learn from this Picture

Standing with the weight all on one foot, or sitting on one foot as girls sometimes do, will injure the shape of the body.

Figure 9-1. Extract from "The Care of the Bones." *The School Journal.*

Another common classroom practice was to require the children to read a passage one at a time in turn around the room – an experience (known as "round robin reading" in the U.S.) that poor readers were apt to find as humiliating as able readers probably found it boring.

Teaching methods for reading were not without their debates, even in these early times. In *A New School Method (Complete)*, (Cowham 1924, 9-21), a textbook prescribed for "pupil teachers" and teachers in training in the 1920s, the author outlines the advantages and disadvantages of the "Alphabetic," "Phonic," "Phonetic," and "Look and Say" methods, and comes down in favor of a "Combined Method."

Writing was taught through the quite separate subjects of handwriting, composition, and spelling. But despite this rather rigid curriculum framework, individual teachers did manage to bring interest and variety to the classroom programs. Although there was no "lan-

Figure 9-2. Nineteenth century New Zealand classroom. Courtesy of Turn-ball Library, Wellington, New Zealand.

guage experience" as a contemporary teacher would know it, teachers were encouraged to do "object lessons," in which an interesting exhibit of some kind was studied in close detail, and were even allowed to indulge in "peripatetics" or experiences and observational visits outside of the classroom or even the school grounds.

One of the problems confronting teachers in these early years was the lack of reading materials. In 1907, to help redress this problem, the Chief Inspector of Schools began the publication of a series of monthly magazines. They were published in three parts (in other words, they were three separate magazines): Part One for five- to eight-year-olds, Part Two for eight- to ten-year-olds, and Part Three for ten- to twelve-year-olds. They were called *The School Journal* (Parts One, Two, and Three), and they were issued free to all public schools throughout the country. Private and secondary schools were able to purchase copies for a half-penny for Part One and a penny for Parts Two and Three.

NEW ZEALAND.—EDUCATION DEPARTMENT.

The School Journal.

PART II.—FOR CLASSES III AND IV.

At least one copy of each Part should be filed in the school as a School Record.

VOL. X.—No. 1.]   WELLINGTON.   [FEBRUARY, 1916.

HOLIDAY-TIME.

Figure 9-3. The cover from *The School Journal* Part Two, February 1916

What was even more remarkable was the fact that for the first 40 years they were issued *to the children* – in other words, every child in a public school received his or her own personal copy of *The School Journal* each month.

In the early years, and especially in schools in remote country districts, *The School Journal* was almost the only reading material available. Little wonder, then, that the monthly arrival and unpacking of *The School Journal* was treated as a major event.

In the beginning, social studies material tended to dominate the content and often this was with a rather heavy-handed attempt to inculcate the virtues of patriotism and loyalty to the British Empire. But in time the journals came more and more to reflect and explore the local New Zealand setting and the authentic experiences of New Zealanders.

There have been changes to the journals over the years. In the late 1940s, due to the postwar paper shortage, the journals ceased to be issued personally to the children and instead became and were stamped the "Property of the School." This was a loss in one sense – having your own copy meant you could go on reading and re-reading the stories long after that particular school year was over – but it did

---

The Arrival of *The School Journal*

The arrival of *The School Journal* was an event in our young lives. The headmaster would enter the classroom with a bundle of shiny white *Journals* under his arm and put them on the teacher's stand. Out would come our *Journal* covers, which would be placed open (without any noise) on the desk in front of us. Row monitors would go to the front of the room, collect enough *Journals* for each child, and distribute them. We then opened the *Journal* at the staples, slipped it under the string in the cover, and it was ours for the rest of the school year. Silence reigned as we explored the new *Journal*, and the room was soon redolent with the characteristic smell fifty *School Journals* gave off when they were opened and their pages turned for the first time. (Smith, M. 1982, 42).

W.L. Renwick – Director-General of Education

The School Library Service

The School Library Service (now the National Library of New Zealand) was established in 1942 to provide curriculum resources for teachers and advisory help with the setting up and running of school libraries. The service continues to this day. Teachers are able to visit, write in, telephone, or fax requests for a selection of high-interest books for their class level or for a range of books on particular topics, and these will be immediately freighted to the school on periods of extended loan. The service is provided free by the Ministry of Education but schools have to pay the return freight costs. Schools may also request help with setting up and running their own libraries. With the advent of new information technology, the National Library of New Zealand has also begun to develop new information services and products for schools. A good example of this is *Index New Zealand*, a CD-ROM reference index to all New Zealand publications which may now be found in secondary school libraries throughout the country.

mean that now schools were able to build up a great store of interesting and innovative reading materials to supplement the classroom reading program.

The loss of the personal ownership of *The School Journal* was perhaps compensated for in other ways, too. By then, books and reading materials were more readily available in the community. Also, in 1942 the School Library Service was established to provide a free library service to schools throughout the country.

Over the years there were format changes to the journals and also a change from monthly to quarterly publication. Teachers have used them in various and changing ways, too. The journals have been used as instructional readers, as a resource for the teaching of social studies, science, even spelling, as a model for writing and publishing, and of course for entertainment and enjoyment. But despite all the changes, both to the journals and to New Zealand schools, the journals have continued to hold an important place in classroom reading programs. Currently there are four parts, each targeted for the abilities and interests of a specific age group. Each issue usually contains a mix of stories, factual articles, and poems, all with lively and provocative illustrations. Sometimes there are puzzles, jokes, and even recipes. Plays for children to perform have been another popular inclusion. From time to time, poems from previous issues have been gathered together for a complete verse issue. Fiction is collected from a number of issues for periodic anthology issues entitled *Now for a Story*. There are also *Junior Journals*, which match the regular issues in format but are geared for even younger children.

The journals have not only delighted children – they have won awards for the quality of their design and illustration and have also launched many a New Zealand writer into print. Margaret Mahy, author of numerous books for children and twice winner of the English Carnegie Medal as well as many other prestigious awards, was first published in *The School Journal. The Lion in the Meadow*, her very first children's book (Mahy 1986b), had begun life as a story in *The School Journal* (Mahy 1965). Another New Zealand *School Journal* author who may be known to U.S. readers is Joy Cowley. James K. Baxter, one of New Zealand's major poets, worked on the journals, and another important New Zealand poet, Alistair Campbell, edited the journals from 1950 to 1959.

The "School Pubs"/U.S. Connection

The School Publications Branch of the Department of Education has its own special connection with the United States. John Melser, a New Zealand teacher and teacher educator who became the editor of "School Pubs" in the 1960s, later moved to New York City to lecture at Hunter College and the Bank Street College of Education. He was invited by a group of parents to organize and run one of the first alternative schools in the public system, Public School #3 in Greenwich Village. He became the headteacher and principal and remained there until his retirement in 1990. The school achieved national recognition for its fresh approach to open classrooms, mixed grades, whole language instruction with books rather than basal readers, and an emphasis on arts as an integral part of education. It was, in effect, a "New Zealand school" in the heart of New York City.

For many years *The School Journal* was produced in Wellington by the School Publications Branch of the Department of Education (known affectionately as "School Pubs"). In 1989, with the restructuring of the administration of the New Zealand Education System, School Publications became Learning Media.

The 1950s: The Janet and John Years

But I am jumping ahead. Back in the 1940s, teachers were able to take advantage of *The School Journal* and the School Library Service to supplement their classroom reading programs, but there was growing dissatisfaction with the boring and meaningless instructional texts being used with beginner readers.

There had been little change since the nineteenth century in the way reading was taught. The approach involved a heavy emphasis on "phonics" and children were taught to "attack" unfamiliar words by "sounding them out," letter by letter in a mechanical fashion, with little regard for meaning or enjoyment. Any attempt to predict (using other strategies such as drawing on context or semantic clues) was frowned on and dismissed as "guessing." (Children often complied by giving the teachers what they seemed to want: I can recall my own first teacher, who was a great believer in the need to "sound out" every letter before saying the word. I can remember on more than one occasion knowing what a word was from context clues but going through the motions of "sounding out" just to keep the teacher happy!)

The growing dissatisfaction with the instructional reading materials of the day led to a committee being set up in 1949 to revise the "infant reading syllabus," as it was then called. As a result of their deliberations, the *Janet and John* reading series was introduced to New Zealand schools. These were English adaptations of the American *Alice and Jerry* basal textbooks (*Dick and Jane* was another variant). Some changes were also made to the illustrations and the vocabulary to match the New Zealand setting. In England, teachers were offered two ways to use the series – one emphasizing phonics and the other through whole word recognition. New Zealand officially opted for the latter (the term of the day was "look and say"), but nonetheless some phonics was taught on the side.

Today's New Zealand teacher would ridicule the *Janet and John* series, but in their time these readers were a considerable advance on what had been available before. Greater attention was paid to interest and children were encouraged to use a wider range of

with

I saw John
and John saw me.
'' Come and play,'' he said.
'' Come and play with me.''

7

Figure 9-4. An illustration from a *Janet and John* book

strategies. They were also supported by a variety of supplementary readers which were produced by commercial publishers. Teachers sent these home with the children each night so that their reading could be "heard" and as a result, a very strong tradition of parent and community involvement in the process of learning to read began to develop.

But while teachers were using *Janet and John* as directed by the Department of Education, the series quickly acquired some stern critics. One of these was Sylvia Ashton-Warner.

In the early 1950s Sylvia Ashton-Warner was teaching in a little country school, miles from any large town and indeed, it seemed, from the rest of the world. Her students were Maori, the indigenous people of New Zealand. Outside of the school, their lives were rich with exciting experiences. They went eeling, walked through long grass, raced each other down hills, climbed trees, kicked sand on the beach, teased brothers and sisters, did chores around the house, helped out on the farm, held babies, spoke to old people, and took part in family rituals.

Yet the *Janet and John* readers supplied by the Department of Education never touched on these things. Although there had been

Figure 9-5. Sylvia Ashton-Warner

an effort to adapt them for New Zealand children, their English origins were clearly there in the illustrations, the content, and even the language. These were stories about white middle-class children who always wore shoes and socks and who lived in a world where you traveled in cars or buses and where it snowed at Christmas time. For Sylvia Ashton-Warner's students all this made no sense and had no connection with their experience of life. Most had never seen snow, and anyway, they celebrated Christmas in the middle of summer. Furthermore, the only travel most of the children ever did was to school and that was on horseback or on foot. They knew about sheep and pukekos and eels – but not the English birds and animals in the *Janet and John* stories. As for shoes and socks, most came to school barefoot – not so much because they were poor but because that seemed the most comfortable and natural thing to do.

Sylvia Ashton-Warner found the children wanted to learn to read, but the Department of Education's books did not catch their imagination. They remained politely but sadly bored. But when she wrote down the things they told her they had experienced or felt, she noted an immediate quickening of interest. Powerful ideas seemed to be triggered by these magical words. They wanted her to read the writing back to them. *They* wanted to read it, too. Suddenly, after laboring for months over the Department of Education's tedious textbooks, the children began to clamor to read and write.

A number of important things were happening here. First, the reading materials made connections with the children's own experiences. The children were able to draw on context and to make predictions, but above all to engage with the ideas and so understand and enjoy the writing. Sylvia Ashton-Warner also showed us how important it was to make seamless connections between reading and writing, talking and reflecting, thinking and imagining.

This educator did another very New Zealand thing – she set her ideas about how children learn in a *story*. (American teachers sometimes comment on how New Zealand educators, when talking about educational theory and practice, often do so by using stories and anecdotes.) Tagging the learning to a memorable story or incident not only enhances it, but it also gives it emotive power and it helps model the learning. Sylvia Ashton-Warner's first novel, *Spinster*, published in 1958, became an international best-seller and following the publication of *Teacher* in 1963, her reputation as a great educational innovator was firmly established. Both novels set learning in a real-life situation and related it holistically to the whole person.

Sylvia Ashton-Warner's impact on New Zealand was complicated. She was a controversial figure – deeply introspective, yet flamboyant and hugely demanding. In the words of her biographer Lynley Hood, "Sylvia sought unconditional love and admiration from her mother country and its Department of Education, and bitterly accused both of rejecting her when her expectations were not met" (Hood 1988).

Another important influence on the emerging holistic curriculum and philosophy was Elwyn Richardson. In 1947 this talented young educator who had first begun to train as a scientist moved to a one-teacher school in the remote and tiny Northland community of Oruaiti. Instead of teaching textbook lessons and trying to impart factual information as laid down by the syllabus, he turned to the natural environment. Together he and the children explored the real world about them. They examined the shells on the beach, measured the growth of plants, catalogued the living creatures, recorded the patterns and rhythms of the weather and the seasons – and they shared their discoveries and their ideas and feelings about their discoveries. They wrote poems and stories, made lino-cuts and paintings, sought out clay from the district, taught themselves pottery, and fired their own creations in a log-fired kiln.

This rich and exciting journey of discovery was documented in

Figure 9-6. Elwyn Richardson

Richardson's book *In the Early World* (Richardson 1964). Much of his approach to education was intuitive and verified by practice, yet so many of the labels that have come to be associated with child-centered learning fit comfortably here. The children were using language in an authentic way. They were discussing, reading, writing, sharing, thinking, problem solving, imagining, and creating. This was an integrated curriculum, with math, science, music, language, art, and social studies all flowing naturally into each other. This was environmental education. This was learner-centered learning, holistic learning, experience-based learning. They were doing real science (paleontology, botany, zoology), not classroom science "activities." The children were using real experiences, not borrowing those of the teacher or the textbook.

The children were so excited about their learning that it didn't stop when they left the school at the end of the day or even at the end of their schooling. Instead, they carried their awareness and their creativity with them. Elwyn Richardson tells the story of one child who developed a passion for Spanish gates. It all began when the children became immersed in a study of gates. It was a country district so there were plenty of gates to study. They started with farm gates and then moved on to study gates around the world and gates through history. The whole class became fascinated by the intricate wrought iron designs brought by the Moors to Spain. Not only the children became caught up in this study – the whole community was suddenly thinking about gates. The local blacksmith was so excited he taught the children how to weld. Years later, Elwyn Richardson returned to the district to take part in a television documentary on his work. Here he met a number of his past pupils, including one who made gates for a living! He had been inspired by the Spanish gates he had studied in his school days and had started to make his own version for the local market. Unfortunately, the demand for Spanish gates was not high, so he usually had to concentrate on making ordinary New Zealand gates. But, as Elwyn Richardson tells it, on Fridays he forgets about ordinary gates and makes Spanish ones!

Elwyn Richardson's emphasis on creativity was not in any sense a wishy-washy acceptance of lazy or imprecise thinking. He was rigorous and expected the children to discipline their talents and ideas in the pursuit of excellence. In their writing, children worked through their drafts, challenging their own achievements and striving to express their ideas and feelings with accuracy, originality, and authenticity.

Four Poems by the Children of Oruaiti

The Rain Gauge Horses

Around and around and backwards and forwards,
The scampering-fit horses gallop and buck,
"It's going to rain," I said
"Horses make good rain gauges."
Whenever it rains their drumming feet can be heard
all over the paddocks.
Their screaming call rings out all over the farms,
Bang, bang, bang, thumpety, thump.
The drum sound feet pattern the paddocks.

Ronny
(Richardson 1964, 105)

Wattle

The wind shorn wattles
Sway wildly today
While the blue gums rattle
Like paper in the cinders.

Ted, age eleven
(Richardson 1964, 92)

Hopscotch

Thump, thump
The stamping of feet
can be heard of the flop-footed people.
And the clack, slap of the flattened tin
Thrown,
And the hooray of the people as the player gets out
And the weary sigh lifts the air
As the player walks away
From the hopscotch patch.

Valerei, age ten
(Richardson 1964, 92)

The gates are shut on the braying cattle,
The doors are shut on the prowling men,
The henhouses are shut on the sleek rats,
And the night is silent for ever more.

Brett, age ten
(Richardson 1964, 217)

Elwyn Richardson's book *In the Early World* was visionary and yet thoroughly practical. It didn't waste time on academic educational debate or theory, yet a rich and challenging philosophy is embodied in the classroom examples he describes. He pushed back the boundaries for child-centered learning and a holistic curriculum, and in this way provided an example and a challenge for the teachers that were to follow him.

Against such vivid and personal learning, the *Janet and John* reading texts began to appear all the more contrived and incongruous. The methodology was increasingly seen as dubious, as well. The "look and say" approach with its reliance on children memorizing "sight words" as a major and sometimes exclusive reading strategy meant that children were frequently at a loss when they encountered unfamiliar language while trying to read things other than their reading texts. The experience with the *Janet and John* series only served to highlight the difference between real reading, where the grasp and

"Barking at Print"

To appreciate the full significance of this phrase one needs to have heard a record that was very popular in this county in the 1950s and which even made it onto the "hit parade" at the time. It is a recording of a group of dogs "barking" "Mary Had a Little Lamb." The conductor of this canine choir had selected dogs with barks of different pitches that happened to match the notes in the nursery rhyme. They were then trained to bark when the conductor pointed at them and the result was "Mary Had a Little Lamb." Of course, they weren't really "singing" the tune, and readers who declaimed memorized sight words without understanding or enjoyment weren't really reading either.

processing of meaning is an integral part, and being able to "say the words," or what Don Holdaway has termed "barking at print."

The 1960s: Enter Ready to Read

Despite the smoldering dissatisfaction with the *Janet and John* series it continued to be used throughout the 1950s. But New Zealand's population was growing rapidly thanks to a postwar "baby boom." By 1959, just to keep schools supplied, a major reprint of the *Janet and John* series was becoming necessary. The question was asked: Why doesn't New Zealand create its own reading series? After due deliberation, the Department of Education, the controlling body for the country's education in those days, decided to take this momentous step and commissioned the School Publications Branch of the Department of Education (School Pubs) to set about preparing and producing what was to become the first series of *Ready to Read* books.

Myrtle Simpson, an experienced teacher and school inspector, was given the task of supervising the development of the series. Before anyone put pen to paper, discussions were held throughout the country as to what was needed. Junior class teachers, curriculum advisers, inspectors, teachers' college and university lecturers, and teacher union groups all contributed. They decided that what they wanted was not a "textbook" or a set of "instructional readers," but a collection of stories and books that would:

◆ Provide a steady progression of difficulty for the teaching of reading to young children;
◆ Include New Zealand content;
◆ Present stories close to the children's experiences;
◆ Enable children to make use of context;
◆ Contain stories to be read at one sitting;
◆ Include language New Zealand children would naturally experience in conversation and in the course of having stories read to them;
◆ Provide a national series;
◆ Provide models for publishers (UNESCO 1984, 39).

Material was then prepared and trialed in 33 schools throughout the country, and when published, was supplied free to all schools. Teachers were greatly assisted by a handbook entitled *Suggestions for Teaching Reading in Infant Classes*, which was prepared by Myrtle Simpson and published by School Publications in 1962.

The *Ready to Read* series was also helped and supported by another major landmark in the development of the learner-centered language curriculum. This was the publication in 1960 of a new syllabus for English teaching in primary schools. Prior to this, the English syllabus had been *prescriptive* – it said what teachers should teach at each class level. But the new syllabus was a major departure in that, in essence, it defined what good language users do and instructed teachers to find where their children were on their way to being good language users and what their needs were, and to set about their teaching from there. It was a clear affirmation of the importance of child-centered learning. Teachers were given additional practical assistance to implement it by a set of three *Handbooks of Suggestions for Teaching English* and through inservice help from an expanded Advisory Service.

The approach of the 1960s syllabus was also strongly *holistic*. It described four language "modes" – speaking, listening, reading, and writing – but made it clear that these were not to be regarded as separate "subjects." Learning was to be integrated and language was to flow across the curriculum. This, however, was not a departure or a new direction, but rather a confirmation of the way many good teachers were already working. It was, in fact, a period of great curriculum ferment and advance, with the publication of other new syllabuses and supporting handbooks in art and craft, social studies, and arithmetic. The Advisory Service was expanded to help and support teachers through these changes.

The 1970s and 1980s: The World Comes to Watch

As teachers began to work with the *Ready to Read* series and the accompanying suggestions for classroom organization and teaching methods, they began to be excited by the results. Surveys that compared the reading competence of New Zealand children with children in other countries reinforced this. But at the same time, teachers were also noting deficiencies and aspects of the series that could be improved. In 1975 the Department of Education undertook a comprehensive evaluation of the series to provide the basis for a complete revision of the books. The demands to be met by the revised series were rigorous.

♦ The emphasis must be on stories which are so interesting that children find them compelling reading.

- If the children are to read for meaning, the stories must be capable of being related to their background of experience.
- The language used must be that which children are likely to have experienced naturally in the course of conversation and in the stories that have been read to and with them – a view summed up in the term "natural language texts."
- The series must provide a manageable gradient of difficulty and challenges in regard to the concepts, language structures, and vocabulary used to develop the theme in each story – a view summed up in the term "graded texts" (UNESCO 1984).

Other points stressed were the need for a wider range of literary forms (such as poems, fables, fantasy, and nonfiction) and to provide better balance in relation to gender roles and greater sensitivity in the handling of various other social and cultural issues.

Texts were called for and manuscripts flooded in from all over the country. Out of more than seven thousand, 150 were ultimately selected for trialing, and of these, some 48 (Ministry of Education 1985, 98-99) were to finally make up the revised and extended *Ready to Read* series under the editorship of Margaret Mooney.

The *Ready to Read* series was not only to be profoundly successful, but it also provided a model for commercial publishers to follow. Drawing on the strengths of the series, Shortland Publications began the *Story Box* series, which was to prove highly successful in the U.S. as well as in New Zealand. *Sunshine Books* quickly found success internationally, too. Ashton Scholastic brought new books into children's homes through its school book clubs, while Scholastic Inc. did the same for children in other countries. These "sons and daughters" of *Ready to Read* were joined in the U.S. by the *Ready to Read* collection itself in 1987, when Richard C. Owen Publishers, Inc. began to distribute the books in the U.S.

Yet, despite the international acclaim for New Zealand's reading programs and the undoubted success in comparative terms, there was still the vexing question: Why do so many children who learn to speak with ease and joy face failure and frustration in learning to read and write? This was the question Don Holdaway has been battling during his long career as teacher, clinician, consultant, researcher, and writer. He is probably best known to teachers in the U.S. for his book *The Foundations of Literacy* (1979), which is frequently prescribed as a text for the academic study of reading. Yet the book is first and foremost the distillation of a lifetime spent in the practical world of the classroom. He wasn't concerned just with children mastering the

Figure 9-7. Don Holdaway

skills and strategies of reading, but also drew attention to the power of the learner's attitude. What he sought to do was to make reading so exciting and enthralling that reading would become a life-long love.

Holdaway had observed how magical the traditional "bedtime story" can be. There is the child, warm and cozy in bed – maybe feeling really snug after a nice warm bath – and sitting beside him or her and probably cuddling the child is one of the most important people in his or her world. And what does this parent or caregiver do? He or she opens a book and begins to read. It's bound to be no ordinary book, either. It'll be a picture book that has been carefully written and wonderfully illustrated. As the story begins to weave its spell, the child becomes engrossed, almost forgetting to breathe. Together, parent and child will linger over the illustrations, share the excitement as the story builds to the page turns, be charmed by the twists and turns of the narrative, and begin to predict and guess what may happen next. So much incidental but important learning is going on here – the child is learning about the direction of the text, about story structure, about how books have a front and a back, and how the language

flows from left to right in sweeps. The child may begin to learn to recognize letters and words and pieces of familiar text. As the child comes
to know the text, he or she may join in with the reading. But most important of all, the child is learning that reading is an exciting, warm,
comforting, important, good thing to be able to do.

After observing all this, the question Don Holdaway asked was –
how can we get that same kind of powerful intimacy in the classroom?
During the 1960s he worked with teachers in the Auckland area to
develop and trial what has come to be known as the "shared book experience" and is now a central part of a balanced reading program in
New Zealand classrooms.

But one of the major barriers to the kind of bedtime story intimacy that Holdaway wanted to achieve was book size – most books
were too small to share in such a close way. His answer was simple –
why not use bigger books? The idea of "big books" quickly caught on
among teachers. At first publishers were slow to follow suit, so what
began to happen all over the country was an amazing example of community publishing (and also, incidentally, breach of copyright!). Parents would be invited to working bees at the school. The teachers
would show the parents the books they wanted to share with the children in this way, and the parents would make an enlarged version –
copying the text and the illustrations onto large pieces of paper. They
called these "blown-up books" and they began to be used all over the
country. It wasn't long before publishers began to realize that this
was an exciting addition to the shared reading process, and they too
began to publish big book versions of their successful stories. Big books
had arrived!

Learners with Special Needs

But with all the best care in the world, children still fail to learn
to read. In their attempts to help these failing children, the traditional
approach has been to provide remedial reading programs. But sadly,
the success rate for these is not high. What tends to happens is that,
as a result of all the remedial help, the children may manage to advance their reading from point A to B, as it were, but meanwhile, their
peer group has moved on to D or E. In other words, once failure has
set in it is very hard to get enough acceleration in the child's learning to make up for the lost ground, so that they never completely catch
up with their peers.

This was one of the problems that Marie Clay wrestled with.

Figure 9-8. Marie Clay

Throughout the 1960s and '70s, starting from the time when the *Ready to Read* books were first introduced, she studied what children were learning about reading and writing in their classroom programs. In addition, she worked with teachers in workshops to encourage them to become more observant of individual children's progress (see Clay 1979). The question she asked was simple. As teachers know very well who their slow progress readers are, is there some way we can help these children *before* this becomes a matter of failure? After conducting major studies of children's success in language learning she was able to come up with simple ways for teachers to identify children early on who are at risk of failing to learn to read and write. She then devised an intervention program for these children. The result was Reading Recovery® – a program that was to receive worldwide acclaim. Today it is used throughout New Zealand, is widely used in the United States, and is also used in Canada, England, and Australia.

Reading Recovery has been tremendously successful. This has been borne out by the extensive research that has accompanied it. However, there are some issues that schools have to decide for themselves. One of these is just how many children do you decide to help?

Reading Recovery[1]

There are three main elements to Reading Recovery.

♦ First, there is the need to identify those children who are making slow progress *early*. To do this, Marie Clay devised the Observation Survey (Clay 1993a). This draws on running records of the child's current reading and a number of short diagnostic tests, including letter identification, concepts about print, word tests, a writing test, and hearing and recording sounds (dictation). Children are tested on or about their sixth birthday, providing a record of progress. This means they will have a year to settle in and adjust to school routines. It also gives teachers an opportunity to evaluate the first year of teaching. Using the children's individual birthdays also means testing will be spread over the whole year rather than all occurring at one time.

♦ Those identified for supplementary help receive intensive individual instruction with a specially trained Reading Recovery teacher. In the daily one-on-one half-hour sessions, the teacher observes what the child does and can do and develops a program of careful and supportive teaching that will foster the reading strategies the child needs. In these sessions, two kinds of learning have to be kept in mind: on the one hand there is fluency and performing with success on familiar material and on the other there is a challenge to achieve independent problem solving in new and interesting texts with supportive teaching. The texts are very carefully selected for the needs of the particular pupil to foster acceleration (Clay 1993b).

♦ The third element is the need to return the child to the normal class program as quickly as possible – partly because that is the goal of the program anyway, but also to prevent the child from becoming dependent on the program (a common problem with traditional remedial programs).[2]

---

[1] In the U.S., Reading Recovery® is a registered trademark of the Reading Recovery Council of America.

[2] For additional information, see Clay, Marie M. 1993. *An Observation Survey of Early Literacy Achievement*. Portsmouth, NH: Heinemann, and Clay, Marie M. 1993. *Reading Recovery: A Guidebook for Teachers*. Portsmouth, NH: Heinemann.

Reading Recovery is an *early* intervention program – this means we cannot be precise or definite about how many of the children we choose to help would have gone on to become reading failures without that help. In other words, Reading Recovery is a kind of "insurance" against failure in literacy learning, and schools have to carefully consider the children they serve in order to arrive at a decision as to how much "insurance" they need to carry. In New Zealand schools, among six-year-olds, approximately one child in four receives Reading Recovery help, and for New Zealand children, this has been found to be a "good cover."

But while in many teachers' minds Marie Clay's name is synonymous with Reading Recovery, her work has also had a much wider and perhaps less overt impact on what happens in New Zealand classrooms. In the first place, the Observation Survey, though useful in itself (and perhaps because it was so useful), also helps reinforce and strengthen assessment measures and practices that are authentic and an integral part of the child-centered, needs-based teaching/learning spiral. Most six-year-olds in New Zealand are put through the Observation Survey. Where the traditional American teacher has tended to associate assessment and evaluation of learning with *testing*, the conventional New Zealand junior class teacher tends to think of methods based on *observation* of authentic behavior. Marie Clay's work served to validate this, but also encouraged teachers to develop strategies and practices that would help them observe with greater rigor and consistency in all areas of the school curriculum.

Marie Clay's work also reinforced the philosophically based reluctance of New Zealand teachers to stigmatize children experiencing reading (and learning) difficulty with classificatory labels such as learning disabled, dyslexic, neurological impairment, and attention deficit disorder. An extensive review of the literature on learning disability led her to conclude:

> The Learning Disability concept which seemed to hold so much promise in the 1960s has been espoused by legal, medical, psychological and educational professionals but research and analysis has not produced a successful definition, effective identification or discriminated this condition from other similar states by etiology, diagnosis, treatment or prognosis. The wide use of such an ill-defined category implies that children are being classified as Learning Disabled when there is no agreement on how they should be helped, scant evidence of programs that work, and little effort to find such programs (Clay 1987a, 170).

In learner-centered classrooms, definitions of learning failure in terms of disability are pointless. Labeling the child may relieve the teacher of ultimate responsibility because it puts the onus (and the blame!) on the child – but it doesn't *help* the child. Children who are having difficulty learning to read or write are "failing" simply because they cannot do what they need to be able to do. Helping them meet those needs is where the teacher's task begins. Clay's work reinforced this thoroughly practical and pragmatic view of learning and remediation and helped reinforce the teaching practices that stem from it. She has always worked very closely with classroom practitioners. In all her work, theory and practice are intertwined, the practice validating the theory, the theory enriching the practice.

The New Zealand culture gives a high priority to effective practice in all walks of life, but this emphasis can have its downside, too. While New Zealand junior class teachers have in the past been very successful in their teaching, they have not always been good at explaining to the community what it is they do and why. Marie Clay's work has helped teachers by giving them a vocabulary and an intellectual framework so that they can talk about how children learn to read and write with clarity and precision, and with this has come greater pride in their professional expertise.

The 1990s and Beyond

And so we come to the 1990s. New Zealand teachers are still learning and improving their craft and the child-centered philosophy of learning continues to develop and evolve. In 1995 a new language syllabus was completed – the first complete revision since 1960 (Ministry of Education 1994a)! It embodies the prevailing beliefs teachers have about language and about how children learn from ages five to eighteen, and it provides for the planning, implementation, and evaluation of children's language growth throughout their school lives. Visiting U.S. teachers marvel at the fact that it can cover so much in only 143 pages!

Part III

What Can We Learn
from Each Other?

Chapter 10

⌷⌷

Through Each Other's Eyes

⌷⌷

Learning From Each Other

To sum up and to provide an appropriate conclusion to this book, I thought it would be interesting and useful to list some of the generalizations a very stereotypical, traditional U.S. teacher might offer after visiting a New Zealand classroom – and to do the opposite, too: to list some of the generalizations a New Zealand teacher might give on visiting a very "traditional" U.S. classroom. Of course we are dealing with generalizations and stereotypes here, but sometimes overstating the issues can help us to recognize that there may be some issues that need to be addressed. In fact, such comparisons can be helpful to teachers in both countries – they help us learn about ourselves, and they remind us that we have much to learn from each other.

What do "Traditional" U.S. Teachers Tend to See When They Visit New Zealand Classrooms?

♦ **They would observe child-centered learning.** The program is devised and modified to meet the individual needs of the child, rather than the child being made to fit the program. This emphasis on an individualized program means that New Zealand teachers don't talk about grade or class level. In the first few years of a child's schooling the children move through from a New Entrant class to Junior 1, then Junior 2, and then Junior 3 – all in the space of about three years. But much of the time the children are quite unaware of what class "level" they're in. Instead they're more likely to tell you they're in Miss Wilson's class or Mr. Tamahana's class. Many schools have multi-age classrooms. A few even group the children completely vertically, with children from ages five to nine or even five to twelve in the same room.

♦ **They would notice that skills are taught when the children need them rather** than when a basal textbook declares they should be introduced, or when an assembly-line curriculum plan declares them necessary. This, of course, is another aspect of child-centered learning.

♦ **They would see "kidwatching" as the main means of assessment (Goodman 1991).** For example, with reading, instead of relying on standardized tests which seek to assess children's skills and knowledge on simulated reading behavior, the New Zealand teachers observe the individual child doing real reading and keep a record of the observed behavior. They look for knowledge about reading, the child's reading skills, the strategies the child uses to put those skills to work, and the child's attitude or how the child feels about reading.

♦ **They would enjoy the exciting, language-enriched classroom environments.** The walls are covered with paintings, stories, captions, collages, murals, wall stories, topic dictionaries, puzzles, idea webs, reports, innovations on stories the children have read, shared stories they have written as a class, and books the children have written and published themselves. And not just the walls. There will be children's work hanging from strings across the room, glued to the windows, flowing out into the corridors. There may be constructions and models that have grown out of story ideas that one has to climb over and environmental creations one is invited to enter, like a bear's cave or a giant spider's web borrowed from a much-loved Charlotte (White 1952). One researcher from the United States described the New Zealand classroom as "print-saturated." Visiting teachers from the United States often comment that their fire marshals would have nightmares if they saw some of these rooms!

♦ **They would observe children being encouraged to work together cooperatively and collaboratively,** as a class and in groups – rather than to compete with each other. (At a workshop I gave in Connecticut for a gathering of reading consultants, I began by giving out copies of my then recently published book *Alas My Albatross is Moulting* (Trussell-Cullen 1991), and I asked them to plan some extension reading and language activities in groups. The book is a collection of rather zany but cooperative group games. As they settled down to plan their ideas on a big sheet of paper, one reading consultant declared: "The first thing we have to do is decide what prizes we're going to give the winners." Then, after a few more minutes, as they began to read through the book, another said in a rather puzzled voice: "I don't think there are any winners in these games...")

♦ **They would understand the emphasis is on children doing real reading and writing** – children reading from real books rather than reading textbooks and doing real writing and becoming real writers instead of practice writing or writing exercises. Teachers from basal classrooms are also amazed to see not a ditto sheet or workbook in sight.

♦ **They would realize that teachers strive to emphasize the positive and give children lots of praise and encouragement,** rather than to correct and regularly draw attention to what children *cannot* do. They want children to enjoy their learning because this will give them the power and enthusiasm to go on and to challenge themselves further. For example, when children make spelling mistakes in their writing, the common practice in New Zealand is not to mark the entire word wrong, but to check (√) the letters and parts of the word the child has correct.

My American School and My New Zealand School

The biggest difference is they have swimming in New Zealand. Also, the teacher is funner. She doesn't have us do worksheets. In America when you're doing worksheets, you have to just sit and write letters and if it starts with a "c" you have to put a "c" down and if it starts with a "d" you put a "d."

In New Zealand every day we do something different. We watched butterflies hatch. We made caterpillars out of chalk, paper, crayons, and dye.

In New Zealand when you do writing, you can just do it all by yourself. We didn't do any real writing in America. Our teacher made us write letters and made us do workbooks and gave us shorter playtimes. We couldn't talk when we worked. I like to talk as we work because it makes it easier to sound out words. My teacher in America said, "You'll have to sound it out in your head."

I've learned to read with little books in New Zealand. We didn't do any reading in America. My American teacher made reading unfun. We had to write letters – a, b, c to do it. My New Zealand teacher has a reading class in her school. Each person gets the same book and they sit and read it and it makes it much easier to get it.

There is more playtime in New Zealand. The only thing I like more about school in America is we have a gym class.

Ted Fuller, age six

Ted spent the first four months of his schooling in the U.S. and the next three months in New Zealand.

What Would New Zealand Teachers Think if They Visited a "Traditional" U.S. Classroom (Especially One with a Basal Reading Program)?

- **They would feel there were teachers doing lots of "instruction."** In fact, books written by educators in the United States use the word *instruction* a great deal. However, instructing children, or "telling" them things, is only one way to bring about learning, and often it is not a very effective way. Parents with teenage children might like to ask themselves how many times they have heard themselves saying to their children: "How many times do I have to tell you to...?" Instruction relies heavily on the teacher being in control. It is an assertion of power and as such has a danger of de-powering the learners (or driving them to be subversive). It also relies heavily on the children being effective or compliant listeners. (I am always amused by the way observing teachers often act when I am giving a classroom demonstration in the United States. The teachers listen and take notes attentively when I am talking to the children or working in an instructional mode. But when I divide the children into groups to work independently, the teachers tend to stop watching and start to talk among themselves. It is as if the "real" part of the lesson is over!) The instruction-driven model also requires students to be passive or to do only the actions prescribed by the teacher.

- **The compartmentalization of learning would worry the New Zealand teacher.** They would not be happy to see language divided up into reading and writing as if they were separate subjects, and sometimes further divided into handwriting, "creative" writing, and spelling. Nor would they like to see learning parceled up into watertight subjects and taught in that way with little opportunity for connections to be made, say, between what the children are learning in science and what they learn in art, or between their reading and their physical education. They would worry at the proliferation of specialist teachers, too, each addressing a "portion" of the child, but seemingly with no one considering the whole child.

- **They would be uncomfortable in classrooms where the reading program was still dependent on basal textbooks and workbooks.** They would reject the underlying premise of a basal reading system – that reading is best taught on the assembly line model, with skills being "fastened on" in the same order and at the same time for all children. They would counter by saying children don't all learn in the same way, they bring different experiences to their language learning, and learning is never ordered and predictably continuous – instead there are breakthroughs and sudden growth spurts and also plateaus of consolidation. But the New Zealand teacher would feel at home in child-centered classrooms and would want to encourage and cheer on other teachers who are bravely moving in that direction.

♦ **They would be very suspicious of the heavy reliance on standardized testing,** no matter how sophisticated and seemingly scientific. They would be concerned about the unnecessary stress, the artificiality (why measure simulated behavior when you can observe and evaluate authentic behavior?), the waste of good learning time spent on testing, and the reliance on only one kind of assessment procedure – the test (and especially the mass-administered, multiple-choice, pencil-and-paper tests).

♦ **They would feel the classrooms were rather bare and teacher-tidy.** They would look at the commercially produced posters and display materials on the walls and say: "But where is the hand and the mind of the child?" They would also look at the children's artwork and say: "But why do you try to make your children draw like commercial artists trying to draw like children?" To illustrate this further: I have been in teachers' classrooms in September at the start of the year, and so often I see the teacher has made a special display for the children and it will say something like: "Miss Pedagogy Welcomes Grade 4!" Now that is a nice touch and I don't want to devalue it. But in its own subtle way it can also be seen as another instance of the teacher as the all-powerful instructor and "owner of the learning." A New Zealand teacher wouldn't begin the year that way. Instead, the teacher would get to work with the children to generate some material of their own to put up on the walls. Note the difference: Miss Pedagogy is telling the children "This is my room but you can rent it for a while." When the children put up their own work they are saying, "This is our room – we all own it and we're all responsible for it."

♦ **They would love the class size!** New Zealand has been grinding its way out of a long recession and class sizes of 30 to 35 children are normal and larger classes still are not uncommon. Sometimes U.S. teachers say you can only have an individualized program with the children working in cooperative groupings if you have small classes. The New Zealand teacher would say: "If you are working with 35 children you have to have cooperative grouping and children able to work independently."

♦ **The New Zealand teacher would be impressed by the public interest and concern about education,** but would worry that the U.S. teacher was not respected enough by the community as a professional in his or her own right and that schools at times seemed almost to be under siege by the community.

♦ **The New Zealand teacher would be very impressed by the energy and the commitment of teachers generally** – the way they seek to learn and grow as professionals by attending conferences and workshops during vacations, by their professional reading, and by their concern for the children in their charge.

Chapter 11

The Beginnings of a Child-Centered Philosophy

A Philosophical Outlook

U.S. teachers often ask, "But how did this child-centered language philosophy and curriculum come about?"

♦ Was it an "approach" that was invented by someone who then went around the country preaching and converting other New Zealand teachers?
♦ Was it discovered by some researcher and then trumpeted throughout the nation in some stunning revolutionary research paper?
♦ Was it imposed from on high by some central education bureaucracy?
♦ Or did it come about as the result of a violent reaction to something that was blatantly not working?

In fact, none of the above apply. There was no single "inventor." It is a philosophy that grew holistically from the discoveries teachers made in their own classrooms and then shared with others. Its beginnings were utterly practical rather than theoretical. In fact, New Zealand teachers are very suspicious of any idea that has not been well and truly proved first and foremost in the classroom. As for the researchers, they tended to come after the practitioners had already satisfied themselves that what they were doing was sound. The researchers helped define and validate the practice, but they didn't invent or create it.

Nor was it imposed from on high. Instead, it developed from the classroom up, and this happened because there has always been a tradition of sharing ideas in New Zealand. New Zealand teachers spend a lot of time in and out of each others' classrooms. They often work together in teams. The term New Zealand teachers have for these teams may cause their counterparts in the United States to smile – they call them "syndicates!" (Teaching as organized crime?) There are informal opportunities for teachers to relate with each other, too. As we have seen, the entire faculty comes together every morning for morning break or "playtime." They may just talk and gossip on a personal and social level, but in this informal atmosphere, professional ideas and views are also passed on.

The sharing of aspirations, enthusiasm, and ideas comes easily in this kind of collaborative environment. In the language field, as in so many other curriculum areas, teachers found what worked and shared their ideas with other teachers – first in their own school, then in their own district, and then – through publication, conferences, and inservice courses – across the whole country. School administrators working in curriculum design and support, such as school inspectors, subject advisers, and teacher trainers, took these ideas on board, too, and helped to formalize and spread them further. They also found connections with the work of researchers and writers in other parts of the world, such as John Dewey, Ken Goodman, and Yetta Goodman from the United States, Frank Smith from Canada, and Margaret Meek from the United Kingdom. In the 1980s Donald Graves came to New Zealand and made a powerful impact at a national conference. New Zealand teachers responded readily to his work on children's writing as well as to the work of other researchers such as Donald Murray from the United States and Brian Cambourne from Australia, not because they represented departures from conventional wisdom, but rather because they reflected a continuation or a refocusing of the prevailing beliefs about the way children learn. As a result, this child-centered language philosophy and curriculum grew as a steady evolution rather than coming about through some cataclysmic curriculum shift or educational "big bang."

However, there were a number of local factors that helped the development of this holistic way of teaching.

♦ **Distance from the rest of the world** was clearly one of these. One is less exposed to the whims and fashions of competitive education when one is a twelve-hour plane flight away from most other countries. Not that distance has stopped New Zealanders from reading and keeping up to date with the latest trends. In fact, if statistics on book sales per head of the population are anything to go by, New Zealanders are among the most avid readers in the world. But distance has meant the rest of the world has largely left us to get on with our own thing and to pick and choose which trends and developments we wish to learn from.

♦ Another contributing factor has been the nature and the quality of the **teacher training**. There are a number of key differences between teacher education in New Zealand and the traditional preparation of teachers in the United States. In the first place, with the exception of a period of severe economic recession earlier this century, elementary school teachers have always been trained in specialist teacher-education institutions rather than at multi-purpose universities where teacher education is just another academic option. Despite various name changes, they have remained institutions that are focused on the needs of teachers, both in terms of preservice training and inservice support.

♦ Perhaps as a result of this, another important feature of New Zealand teacher education has always been a strong emphasis on the **practical needs of the classroom**. Professional training is not an "add-on" that students do after completing a number of studies in other academic areas, but an integrated part of the whole course. Much of the training is classroom based and throughout their three to four years of study, students spend regular periods of time working in the classroom alongside experienced mentor teachers.

♦ The New Zealand tradition has always been to prepare teachers for primary schools as **generalists** – competent to teach all subjects: language (including oral, written, and visual language), science, mathematics, social sciences, health, art, music, physical education, information technology, Maori studies, and even swimming. Such an all-inclusive preparation for teaching also helps explain why New Zealand teachers have no difficulty integrating the school subjects and encouraging learning across the curriculum.

♦ Another key factor: New Zealand has always had a **national system of education** with a national curriculum and set of core syllabuses. As a result, a child can move from a school in Invercargil (at the bottom of the South Island) to a school in Kaitaia (near the top of the North Island) without experiencing a major dislocation in academic progress. This is not because the Kaitaia class is likely to be studying the same topics as the class in Invercargil. In fact, that is most unlikely because there is no uniformity of *content* in New Zealand schools. But there is a consistency of *philosophy*, a consistency in the way teachers teach and the way the children are expected to learn. Because of this, there is an easy compatibility between classroom and classroom, school and school, district and district.

♦ This **philosophical consensus** has probably been the most important force that has helped this evolutionary process. As we have seen in the five New Zealand classrooms we have visited in earlier chapters, each teacher may have a unique and individual teaching style, but what unites them and gives them great strength are the beliefs they have in common about the way children learn, about what children should learn and when, and about the best ways teachers can help facilitate that learning. Observers visiting New Zealand often focus on teacher and learner *behavior* – as if "child-centered learning" is something the teacher *does*. But this preoccupation with the practice overlooks the important part played by this consensus philosophy of education. What a teacher believes begets what the teacher does.

Consensus beliefs about literacy teaching and learning in New Zealand classrooms are succinctly stated in the introduction to *Dancing with the Pen: The Learner as a Writer* (Ministry of Education 1992, 6).

New Zealand Teachers' Beliefs About Literacy Learning and Teaching

♦ Reading and writing experiences should be "child centred."
♦ Reading and writing for meaning are paramount.
♦ Writing should have purpose and meaning.
♦ Literacy learning must always be rewarding.
♦ Reading and writing are inseparable processes.
♦ Children learn to read and write by reading and writing many different kinds of texts.
♦ Reading and writing are powerful tools for learning.
♦ Reading and writing fulfil a variety of functions.
♦ The best approach to teaching reading and writing is a combination of approaches.
♦ Good first teaching is essential for continuing success in reading and writing.
♦ The foundations of literacy are laid at home in the early years.
♦ Reading and writing flourish in a supportive community.
♦ Success at reading and writing encourages further reading and writing.

Another statement of consensus beliefs about the teaching and learning of language (including all its strands: oral, written, and visual) is set out clearly in the 1995 syllabus, and of course, the two sets overlap (Ministry of Education 1994a).

♦ Language expresses identity.
♦ Language is fundamental to thinking and learning.
♦ Language is essential for living in society.
♦ Language programs should be learner-centred.
♦ Language development is fostered by an environment which encourages creativity and experimentation.
♦ Language development is fostered by an environment which provides challenges and high expectations for students.
♦ Language learning is dynamic and progressive.
♦ Language learning requires interaction and active participation.
♦ Language is best developed when students understand and control the learning processes.
♦ Language is best developed through an integrated approach to learning.
♦ Language and knowledge about language develop principally through use.
♦ English programs should reflect the New Zealand [i.e., the national and local cultural] context.
♦ Critical thinking is important for learning and language development.
♦ Assessment involves evaluation of students in the process of learning.

Lastly, and perhaps most significant of all, the philosophy of learning that underpins what happens in New Zealand schools is imbued with a deep and abiding valuing of people. In the school setting this means that children are valued as "people" too – not just for their potential or what educators hope they might become – but also for what they are now. In a child-centered classroom, the children are active learners, keen to engage with life in all its diversity. They draw on their own experiences because they are valued and this also empowers and enables them to share in other's experiences, including those of their classmates, their teachers, their communities, and their culture. They have high expectations for themselves and their teachers and as a result take increasing responsibility for their own learning.

Teachers foster these attitudes, not only by what they teach and the way they teach, but also by the way they view what they do themselves as professionals. The focus is not on what we as *teachers* do so much as on what our *students* do and how we manage and facilitate that. Rather than talk about "teaching students," they talk about learners learning. Rather than "tell," they model. Rather than seeking to control the learning, they seek to facilitate and manage it and to encourage self-control. All these subtleties of emphasis come from a philosophy that values people, that celebrates their diversity of experiences, that applauds the unique array of gifts and qualities children bring with them to the classroom, and that cherishes their common humanity. There is a Maori proverb that states:

> *Maku i ki atu he aha te mea nui o te Ao Naku i Whakahokia*
> *he tangata, he tangata, he tangata.*
> (If you ask what is the most important thing in the world,
> it is people, it is people, it is people.)

In Conclusion

In this book we have sought to provide a kind of snapshot of New Zealand education and to give some idea of the history and the cultural forces that have helped shape it. But snapshots are fixed in time and New Zealand society, like that of the United States, is dynamic and continually changing and evolving. It is a sobering paradox that the one thing that is constant in the world today is change. Indeed, change is not only constant, but it is constantly accelerating.

There was a time when an education was seen as an apprenticeship that prepared you for life: what you learned in school was supposed to last you the rest of your days. Not any more. The children we teach will have experiences and problems to deal with that we cannot conceive of and will need knowledge and skills that currently do not even exist. They will change their roles and careers many times in their lives and they will constantly need to redefine themselves in the process. They will have access to a mountain of information and data that seems to be expanding faster than our capacity to grasp and retain it.

In short, learning has become a life-long necessity. Businesses now thrive or fail on how fast they can learn and change. The gurus of the corporate world talk about organizations becoming "learning enterprises." Political commentators talk about the need for a "learning community." Our world has become learner-centered, too. To be a teacher at this time is to be working in one of the most challenging, daunting, exhausting, and exhilarating professions.

We began this book with a quotation from Marshal McLuhan, about fish not knowing they live in water. In the course of this narrative we have at times compared and contrasted aspects of what happens in New Zealand and U.S. classrooms. The purpose has not been to show that one is necessarily "better" or "superior" to the other. To make those kind of value judgments, one needs to refer to one's teaching philosophy and one's belief about the nature of learning and how best to facilitate it. Nor is the implication that U.S. teachers should adopt the "New Zealand model" and mechanically seek to apply it "as is." Education is steeped in culture, and our cultures, although similar in many ways, are significantly different, too.

But comparisons do help us see what we are doing in a new way. Fish may not know they live in water, but what if the fish venture from their familiar waters? We hope the U.S. educators journeying with us through this book to these new and perhaps somewhat different waters will have not only learned about the New Zealand system of education and its philosophy and practice, but that the experience will help them in a positive and fertile way to continue to re-examine and reappraise their own.

References and Further Reading

Ashton-Warner, Sylvia. 1958. *Spinster*. New York, NY: Simon & Schuster.

——. 1963. *Teacher*. New York, NY: Simon & Schuster.

Beyer, E. 1937. "Jump or Jiggle." In Lucy Sprague Mitchell, ed., *Another Here and Now Story Book*. London, England: E.P. Dutton.

Bissex, Glenda L. 1980. *GNYS AT WRK: A Child Learns to Write and Read*. Cambridge, MA: Harvard University Press.

Butler, Andrea and Jan Turbill. 1987. *Towards a Reading Writing Classroom*. Portsmouth, NH: Heinemann.

Butler, Dorothy and Marie M. Clay. 1987. *Reading Begins at Home*. Portsmouth, NH: Heinemann (second edition; North American adaptation by Bobbye Goldstein).

Calkins, Lucy M. 1983. *Lessons from a Child*. Portsmouth, NH: Heinemann.

——. 1986. *The Art of Teaching Writing, first edition*. Portsmouth, NH: Heinemann.

——. 1991. *Living Between the Lines*. Portsmouth, NH: Heinemann.

Cambourne, Brian. 1988. *The Whole Story: Natural Learning and the Acquisition of Literacy in the Classroom*. Auckland, New Zealand: Ashton Scholastic.

Chandler, Sandra. 1992. *When Attempting to Achieve a Goal*, from ideas developed and trialled by teachers at St. Thomas's Primary School, Junior Syndicate.

Clay, Marie M. 1975. *What Did I Write?* Portsmouth, NH: Heinemann.

——. 1979. *Reading: The Patterning of Complex Behaviour, second edition*. Auckland, New Zealand: Heinemann.

——. 1985. *The Early Detection of Reading Difficulties, third edition*. Portsmouth, NH: Heinemann.

—. 1987a. "Learning to be Disabled." *New Zealand Journal of Educational Studies*, Volume 22, number 2, p 170.

—. 1987b. *Writing Begins at Home: Preparing Children for Writing Before They Go to School*. Portsmouth, NH: Heinemann.

—. 1991. *Becoming Literate: The Construction of Inner Control*. Portsmouth, NH: Heinemann.

—. 1993a. *An Observation Survey of Early Literacy Achievement*. Portsmouth, NH: Heinemann.

—. 1993b. *Reading Recovery: A Guidebook for Teachers in Training*. Portsmouth, NH: Heinemann.

Cowham, Joseph H. 1924. *A New School Method (Complete)*. London, England: Westminister School Book Depot.

Cowley, Joy. 1983. *Greedy Cat*. Wellington, New Zealand: Learning Media for Ministry of Education.

Gentry, J. Richard. 1982. "An Analysis of Developmental Spelling in *GNYS AT WRK*." *Reading Teacher*, November, pp 192–199.

—. 1987. *Spel... is a Four-Letter Word*. Portsmouth, NH: Heinemann.

Glover, Ennis. 1987. *The Magpie*. Auckland, New Zealand: Century Hutchinson.

Goodman, Ken, Yetta M. Goodman, and Wendy Hood. 1989. *The Whole Language Evaluation Book*. Portsmouth, NH: Heinemann.

Goodman, Yetta M. 1985. "Observing Children in the Classroom." In A. Jaggar and M.T. Smith-Burke, eds., *Observing the Language Learner*. Newark, DE: International Reading Association and Urbana, IL: National Council of Teachers of English.

—. 1991. "Informal Methods of Evaluation." In J. Flood, J.M. Jensen, D. Lapp, and J.R. Squire, eds., *Handbook of Research on Training the English Language Arts*. New York, NY: Macmillan.

Graves, Donald H. 1983. *Writing: Teachers and Children at Work*. Portsmouth, NH: Heinemann.

Herrigel, Fugen. 1989. *Zen and the Art of Archery*. New York, NY: Vintage Books.

Holdaway, Don. 1979. *The Foundations of Literacy*. Portsmouth, NH: Heinemann.

—. 1984. *Stability and Change in Literacy Learning*. Portsmouth, NH: Heinemann.

Holmes, Janet. 1982. *Language for Learning: Education in the Multicultural School*. Wellington, New Zealand: Department of Education.

Hood, Lynley. 1988. *Sylvia! The Biography of Sylvia Ashton-Warner*. Auckland, New Zealand: Viking.

Kasten, Wendy C. and Barbara K. Clarke. 1993. *The Multi-Age Classroom: A Family of Learners*. Katonah, NY: Richard C. Owen Publishers.

Mahy, Margaret. 1965. "The Lion in the Meadow." *School Journal, Part 1, number 3*. Wellington, New Zealand: Department of Education.

—. 1969. *Dragon of an Ordinary Family*. London, England: Heinemann.

—. 1986a. *When the King Rides By*. Sydney, Australia: Martin Educational/Ashton Scholastic.

—. 1986b. *The Lion in the Meadow*. London, England: Dent, 1986.

Meek, Margaret. 1982. *Learning to Read*. London, England: The Bodley Head.

Meeks, Arone Raymond. 1991. *Enora and the Black Crane*. Sydney, Australia: Ashton Scholastic.

Ministry of Education of New Zealand. 1985. *Reading in Junior Classes*. Wellington, New Zealand: Learning Media.

—. 1992. *Dancing with the Pen: The Learner as a Writer*. Wellington, New Zealand: Learning Media.

—. 1993a. "A Wild Rumpus." *Music Education for Young People*. Wellington, New Zealand: Learning Media.

—. 1993b. *The New Zealand Curriculum Framework*. Wellington, New Zealand: Learning Media.

—. 1994a. *English in the New Zealand Curriculum*. Wellington, New Zealand: Learning Media.

—. 1994b. *Beginning School Mathematics: A Guide to the Resource*. Wellington, New Zealand: Learning Media.

Mooney, Margaret. 1988. *Developing Life-long Readers*. Wellington, New Zealand: Learning Media.

—. 1990. *Reading To, With, and By Children*. Katonah, NY: Richard C. Owen Publishers.

Munsch, Robert. 1989. *The Paper Bag Princess*. Willowdale, Ontario, Canada: Annick Press.

Murray, Donald M. 1968. *A Writer Teaches Writing: A Practical Method of Teaching Composition*. Boston, MA: Houghton Mifflin.

—. 1984. *Write to Learn*. New York, NY: Holt, Rinehart and Winston.

—. 1989. *Expect the Unexpected: Teaching Myself – and Others – To Read and Write*. Portsmouth, NH: Heinemann and Boynton/Cook.

National Commission on Excellence in Education. 1984. *A Nation at Risk*. Cambridge, MA: USA Research.

New Zealand Education Department. 1916. "The Care of the Bones." *The School Journal*, Volume X, number 1, April, pp 44–45.

Parsons, John. 1990. *The One that Got Away*. Petone, New Zealand: Nelson Price Milburn.

Richardson, Elwyn. 1964. *In the Early World*. Wellington, New Zealand: New Zealand Council for Educational Research.

Routman, Regie. 1988. *Transitions: From Literature to Literacy*. Portsmouth, NH: Heinemann.

—. 1991. *Invitations: Changing as Teachers and Learners K – 12, first edition*. Portsmouth, NH: Heinemann.

Simpson, Myrtle. 1962. *Suggestions for Teaching Reading in Infant Classes*. Wellington, New Zealand: School Publications Department.

Smith, Frank. 1978. *Reading*. Cambridge, MA: Cambridge University Press.

—. 1981. *Writing and the Writer*. New York, NY: Holt, Rinehart and Winston.

Smith, John W. A. and Warwick B. Elley. 1995. *Learning to Read in New Zealand*. Katonah, NY: Richard C. Owen Publishers.

Smith, Margaret. 1982. "Tales Out of School." *Education*, Number One, p 42.

Traill, Leanna. 1993. *Highlight My Strengths: Assessment and Evaluation of Literacy Learning*. Crystal Lake, IL: Rigby.

Trussell-Cullen, Alan. 1991. *Alas My Albatross is Molting and Other Great Games*. Crystal Lake, IL: Rigby.

—. 1994. *What Ever Happened to Times Tables? Every Parent's Guide to New Zealand Schools*. Auckland, New Zealand: Reed.

UNESCO Regional Office of Education in Asia and the Pacific. 1984. *Textbooks and Reading Materials, Volume 1*. Wellington, New Zealand: Department of Education.

White, E. B. 1952. *Charlotte's Web*. New York, NY: HarperCollins.

Yarrow, Peter and Leonard Lipton. 1962. "Puff (the Magic Dragon)." New York, NY: Papamar Music Corp.

Most titles were originally published in New Zealand; U.S. edition information is provided here for the reader's convenience.

Index